On Your Own

Adult Independence For Ages 18-100

James Stallone, Ph.D.
Linda Stallone

Upshur Press
Dallas, PA

ON YOUR OWN
Adult Independence for Ages 18-100
By
James Stallone, Ph.D.
Linda Stallone

Library of Congress Cataloging-in Publication Data

Stallone, James, 1937-
  On your own : adult independence for ages 18-100 /
James Stallone, Linda Stallone.
    p. cm.
  Includes bibliographical references and index.
  ISBN 0-912975-11-3 (pbk.) : $11.95
  1. Adulthood. 2. Maturation (Psychology) 3. Family
4. Consciousness. 5. Co-dependence (Psychology)
I. Stallone, Linda, 1947- . II. Title
HQ799.95.S73   1992
155.6—dc20

                                        91-32157
                                           CIP

Publisher's Note—This publication is designed to provide accurate and authoritative information in regard to the subject matter covered. It is sold with the understanding that the publisher and authors are not engaged in rendering psychological, financial, legal, or other professional services. If expert assistance or counseling is needed, the services of a competent professional should be sought.

Published by Upshur Press, P.O. Box 609,
Dallas, Pennsylvania 18612-0609
Communications to the authors can be addressed to the publisher.
Cover photo - Bob Malloy

Acknowledgements

The authors wish to thank the following people who assisted in so many different ways during the publication of this book.

Special thanks to our adult children, Anthony and Maria, whose candid and often confrontational insights, observations, and challenges helped make this book practically realistic as well as theoretically sound.

Sincere appreciation to Ola Mae Schoonover and Anthony Stallone for their skills in desk-top publishing, editing, and book design.

For literary help in the preparation of the manuscript we are particularly grateful to Dr. Regina Kelly, RSM. We also thank Gloria Bubblo, Mike Burnside, Pat and Mary Ann Cleary, Ed and Sally Lottick, Sy Migdal, Harold Rosenn, Ed Schechter, Bob and Karen Shaw, and Susan Sordoni whose suggestions, expertise, thoughtful comments, and support during the various stages of the manuscript have helped improve the book.

We thank the many people we have worked with over the years who inspired us through their courage and determination to become independent adults. Finally, we applaud all those who continue to do their best to ensure an environment in the spirit of the Declaration of Independence where it is possible to be **On Your Own**.

"Can't I just stay here with you and Mom? I don't
like what I've seen of the real world."

Drawing by H. Martin; ©1989
The New Yorker Magazine

Table of Contents

1   *Chapter One*
Growing Up At
Any Age.

25   *Chapter Two*
Building Blocks and
Stumbling Blocks

63   *Chapter Three*
Rolling Out or Rolling
Up the Welcome Mat.

87   *Chapter Four*
Entitlements and
Education:
A Hard Line on the
Bottom Line.

115   *Chapter Five*
Handling Difficult
Situations

171   *Chapter Six*
Adulthood and the
Expansion of Awareness.

189   *Appendix*
Quick Starts to
Independence

197   *Bibliography*

199   *Index*

Chapter One
Growing Up At Any Age

The first chapter of **On Your Own** challenges the assumption that age and adaptability in society ensure adulthood. Expanding current accepted definitions of adulthood and its purpose, Chapter One distinguishes between dependent and independent living.

The differences between growth that is arrested and behavior that is regressed, and between rebellion and independence, are explored. Readers learn why it is necessary to help themselves and others give up old roles and become adults.

Some troubling trends and society's role in fostering overprotection and discouraging independence introduces the need for a radical approach that questions the "sacred cows" of society. The chapter concludes with the differences in the approach presented in **On Your Own** with that of co-dependency literature and programs.

Recently a friend of ours came to a sudden realization concerning his son who is a freshman in college. The Christmas vacation was over, and it was time for his son to return to school. Our friend saw his son off at the airport on a flight the father had arranged and paid for. A few hours later he got a telephone call at home from his obviously peeved son. In a state of annoyance, the young man complained that the connecting flight was late, and he would have to wait three hours at the airport– "What am I going to do?" His father suggested he check to see if he could transfer to another available flight. His son angrily hung up the telephone.

About twenty minutes later, the father got another call from his son who said there were no other flights; he would have to wait the three hours. At this point the son said, in a rising state of frustration, "Well, what am I going to eat?" At that moment the father realized that his son, though in college and mature in so many ways, was still a dependent adolescent. Despite his growing maturity, he was far from fully being an adult. Since our friend knew his son had $20 in his pocket because he had given it to him before the flight, he told him the obvious, "Buy something to eat at the airport snackbar."

Here we're talking about someone who is certainly not a child. We're talking about a young man who is eighteen years old. But in these particular circumstances, he is still living the role of a child. We realize the scenario is being reenacted with varying scripts across America today. Both parents and children need to take a fresh look at the continuing condition of dependency.

As we delved into the matter further we discovered that age eighteen was just the beginning of the phenomena. Further examination revealed that independent adulthood frequently is missing not only in young people, but also in the middle aged and the elderly. Indeed, it could go on to age one hundred. But there is an alternative approach and a better way to become mature adults and relate to those around us. Becoming fully adult is the key transformation that needs to occur regardless of how old we are or what our life circumstances may be.

Dependency doesn't just occur within the 18 to 25 year old group and their parents. We have a vivid recollection of a situation encountered in counseling some years ago. Three middle aged children approached us concerning their 85 year old father, Hugo. Hugo and his wife of sixty years were on the verge of separation. The grown children were distraught because if this happened, they feared "the family would fall apart."

Hugo, as it turned out, had been an "old country" tyrant in his relationship with his wife. He insisted upon getting his way all the time and when he didn't, he would badger, threaten, and manipulate until he did. His wife had put a stop to his dramatic physical threats early in the marriage when she waved a large kitchen knife in front of him and told him if he carried out his threats to physically abuse her she would run him through. He stopped threatening.

In recent years he had told his wife he would cut her off financially if she continued to go places without him, such as weekends away with family or her friends. His wife discovered that there was no way he could legally cut her off financially, and she called his bluff on that one, too. Now he threatened divorce and his wife told him, "If that's what you want, I'll see you in court." Foiled again—only this time Hugo became depressed. He had run out of threats.

An historical review of Hugo's life from his grown children revealed that as a child he had literally hung onto his mother's apron strings. He stayed at home during his teenage and young adult years, and he brought his young bride into the fold, living at the family homestead. Being gifted in his trade, he was offered several lucrative positions outside his home town, but he could never bring himself to leave. Several independent business opportunities passed him by as well.

Eventually Hugo and his young family moved into their own place in the same town, but his controlling pattern of behavior towards others remained much the same throughout his life. Retirement, especially when leaving home for the south in the winters, was such an anxiety-laden experience that he couldn't make the annual trip without taking tranquilizers and blaming his wife because she was the one who wanted to escape the winters. In short, he had resisted being "on his own" all his life—still a child emotionally, and he acted it.

His grown children came to understand that their father's recent dilemma and his pleading with them to intervene with his wife or at least take his side in the altercation was a manifestation of his dependency. He was, in effect, asking them to parent him. They withdrew from the dispute between him and his wife, and they recommended individual and marital counseling. Hugo reluctantly agreed to try counseling complaining that he was too old to change, but he went and began to face his fears. Surprisingly for a man of 85 years, Hugo made steady progress in backing up and growing up, which most significantly showed in a more tolerant relationship with his wife.

We emphasize that being "On Your Own" is no easy matter. Initially, it can be a scary and disturbing experience for the majority of people. Even an older individual tentatively trying new activities can experience apprehension, much like a small child who lets go of physical support, stands on his own for the first time, and experiences a wave of fear.

However, just as the small child soon feels another wave, one of freedom and independence unlike anything experienced before, so can the older person. The results are well worth the effort, because no fear is ever overcome by avoiding it. Our admiration goes out to those who are letting go and standing more and more on their own.

In the natural process of growing up, if certain developmental tasks are not completed, a person might not proceed to the stage of becoming an independent adult. The arrested condition makes it difficult or even impossible for young people to make a clean and complete psychological break from their parents. In this way, people are kept from growing naturally to the adult stage of life, no matter how many years they accumulate chronologically. Often the elderly are not arrested at a childhood stage, but rather they regress or return to a childhood stage because of some significant changes in their lives.

In the past, there have always been people who failed to become separate, adult individuals, but the condition today is rampant in America because of a unique combination of circumstances. Our society has rapidly advanced sociologically, technologically, and economically in the past two generations. Not only do we live longer, it seems we have also extended childhood-adolescence.

Not too long ago, adolescence generally was thought to end between fourteen and sixteen years of age. We can still find many people who dropped out of school and went out to work in their early teens or married—never having had the opportunity to finish high school. Now it's not only the norm to finish high school, but often to finish college as well. Today, many young people expect to go to college, and parents have assumed certain responsibilities for them while they get their education. That is merely one factor that has actually pushed dependency well into the twenties.

We aren't suggesting the elimination of the developmental stage known as adolescence. Nor are we writing off the value of higher education. We recognize the necessity for education and for this period of growth. What we observe as unnecessary is the lengthy protraction (or in some cases permanent arrest) of the stage of development known as adolescence to the detriment of parents, their children, and society.

Immature behavior can occur in anyone at any age from 18 to 100. It makes no difference whether the person is a parent or a child, married or single, older or younger. At the basis of inappropriate and immature behavior is either an **arrest** at an earlier stage or a tendency to **regress** to earlier stage behavior when under stress. Our premise is that growth or maturation need <u>never</u> stop because life is evolutionary and it is a continuing process. Not only can the young continue to grow and mature, but so can the elderly.

People whose growth is arrested or regressed never grew up or grew out of a particular stage of life. Perhaps their parents protracted or prolonged their dependency so long they were unable to break away from the parents. Instead of going through life as adults, they may have married and transferred their dependency from their parents to their spouses, expecting to be taken care of in the new relationship as their parents had taken care of them in the past.

Distinguishing Dependent from Independent Living

The word "necessity" comes to mind when we think of dependency. People require food, clothing, shelter, rest, and exercise—these are necessities. To some degree everyone is dependent on others for the provision of physical necessities, and few if any of us are totally self-sufficient. But we are not referring to this kind of dependency in **On Your Own**. We are talking about people who become dependent on others for necessities that they can, to some extent, provide for themselves. They create the unwarranted necessity of a caregiver and put the responsibility for their necessities on someone else. Others now have the "obligation" to provide necessities for the dependent people—necessities for which the dependent persons are "response-able" or capable of providing themselves.

Many people not only put responsibility for physical necessities on others, but they also assign responsibility to others for making them feel good in general and in particular for making them feel good about themselves. Dependent people who place themselves at the mercy of others in this way see themselves as potential victims. When this occurs, they can only respond to the situation by "reacting," rather then seeing themselves as initiators of action. The results are feelings of helplessness and the experience is one of "inertia," rather than progress or growth.

Likewise, when people make themselves indispensable as caregivers, they often do so by using fear or guilt to put obligations on the dependent person to stay in the relationship as a way of maintaining the status quo. Whether the caregiver or the care-taker dominates the relationship, the result is a prison in which both feel trapped because they are both dependent. Such relationships are filled with expectations and irrational "shoulds," "oughts," and "musts." There is much blaming and complaining, and aloneness is experienced as loneliness.

Independent people, on the other hand, also desire the basic necessities such as food, clothing, etc., but they accept the "need" to be "responsible" and to provide for themselves to whatever extent they can. Independent people see themselves as response-able and they perform action in accordance with their needs. Thus the emphasis shifts to need and its implied "respond to" and away from necessity and its implied "obliged to." Independent people now have taken matters into their own hands through "action," and they are potential victors, not victims.

Independent people are capable not only of providing their own basic necessities but also of feeling good about themselves by themselves. If they desire to be in a relationship (or desire anything else for that matter), independent people create a need to act and see themselves capable of responding. Their lives and relationships are characterized by excitement and "growth." Thus, we can associate the words necessity, obligation, reaction, and inertia with dependence and the words need, responsibility, action, and growth with independence.

Being independent and **On Your Own** assumes the existence of the potential, opportunity, and relative freedom to do so. This assumption does not always apply for those who are physically or mentally disabled or for those who live under political, social, and economic oppression. Their difficulties are addressed in other forums and by other means. We can only encourage those in such circumstances to do all they can for themselves, to whatever extent they can. **On Your Own** is addressed to the majority of people who are physically and mentally able and who live in democratic, developed societies where opportunities and freedom are available.

We have tremendous compassion for people who are coping with overcoming immature behavior patterns and who are moving to a new stage of development. We do not, however, subscribe to the idea that any stage of development is particularly the most difficult; there are difficulties at every stage of growth. For example, just being born is traumatic, as is the first experience of parting with parents and going to school; puberty and the accompanying psycho-sexual changes are disruptive. Getting married and having children; the famous mid-life crisis; retirement; dying and death. All of these present their own special difficulties and developmental tasks that need to be accomplished. But any of these circumstances are more complicated when the key players involved are held back by ingrained immature tendencies.

Arrested Growth and Dependency

Arrested growth in adolescents could result from a failure to declare independence from parents, perhaps because they felt unable to declare their independence out of fear, or they could not make a clean break from overprotective or possessive parents and then later from the parent-substitutes. The case of Marcia illustrates growth that has been arrested.

When Marcia came for therapy, she needed to understand the effects of having had an overprotective mother. Marcia typified the obedient, dependent child when she was growing up, the child who went through the early stages of her life without ever a whimper of rebellion or dissent. She married a domineering and abusive man and remained the same child in her relationship with him as she did with her mother. Finally at age 48, she asked her husband of twenty-eight years to leave after he physically abused her one time too often. He was so confident she could not get along without him that he left in order to scare her.

Luckily Marcia came for help at that time and managed, though fearfully, to get a job, go back to school, file for a divorce, and insist that their house be sold and profits split.

Marcia adjusted to living alone and was no longer afraid to even go to bed by herself, literally! She had finally begun to grow up. Marcia's husband subsequently was impressed with the changes that had taken place in her. He asked her if he could come back. After an appropriate courtship, she was satisfied that he really had "cleaned up his act," and they renewed their wedding vows, or in this case, **consciously** took those vows for the first time.

Regressed Behavior and Dependency

Regression to immature behavior is another common occurrence, particularly when a person is undergoing a stressful experience. While a significant degree of independence may have already been achieved by an individual, a major life stressor causes the person to retreat to less mature and dependent behavior in order to cope with the situation. The following case involving Mildred, aged 71, is a case in point.

Mildred's husband died and left her alone, but financially secure. Their relationship had been a traditional marriage, her husband assuming the role of protector and provider and she as homemaker and nurturer. Their roles were very circumscribed with little overlap. He could not fry an egg, and she could not mow the lawn.

Mildred fell apart emotionally after her husband's funeral, and her well-meaning daughter-in-law took her into her home. Mildred's condition worsened as her daughter-in-law did more and more for her. She lay around the house and either pouted or cried whenever she was asked to do anything. Soon after returning to her part-time job, her daughter-in-law came for counseling in exasperation because she feared leaving Mildred alone. When the daughter-in-law had left the house for work from 7 A.M. to 3 P.M., she returned home only to find that a sulking Mildred had not eaten all day because no one was there to cook and serve her.

The daughter-in-law considered quitting her job to take care of her helpless mother-in-law, even though she was sure that Mildred was perfectly capable of feeding and taking care of herself. We introduced the daughter-in-law to the principles in this book and on the basis of a more complete understanding of Mildred's behavior, she was prepared to "nip this childish behavior in the bud" before the pattern went any further. The daughter-in-law told Mildred to cook and serve herself while she was at work.

The first day Mildred did not eat. The daughter-in-law did not relent. Knowing her daughter-in-law meant business, the second day, when Mildred got hungry enough, she prepared her own lunch. This was a major turning point for Mildred who then progressively did more and more for herself. With the help and understanding of her daughter-in-law, Mildred came to appreciate the principles of growth operating in her own life. She was able to see how dependencies cultivated over years were behind her own resistance to change. Mildred finally accepted the idea that it was time to move into a senior citizens apartment complex. She fared quite well in her new environment and one evening she even had an interested gentleman over for a gourmet dinner that she cooked herself!

Helping Others Become Adults

The protraction of adolescence so prevalent today breeds into people an excessive sense of dependence and entitlement. Once fostered, it is not a difficult leap to the mentality where young people, and even middle aged or elderly people, perceive parents, teachers, or college administrators, government officials, social service workers and medical professionals from the viewpoint of, "What more should they do for me?" This sense of entitlement and its satisfaction actually prevents those who are dependent from ever becoming complete and independent adults. And again, we emphasize that chronological age is irrelevant.

In this regard, the people most in need of hearing our message are the newly affluent. Too often they cling to the notion that they don't want their children to go through the same struggles they experienced or the disadvantages they grew up with. They allow their children to have what they didn't have without asking or working for it or even knowing what it cost. Consequently, they end up giving the children everything and denying them the chance to learn how to achieve and experience independence themselves.

Parents who continue to supply adolescents with everything are doing neither themselves nor their children a service. Not only are parents burdened with never-ending bills and the responsibility of parenting beyond reasonable needs, but the parents are hampered in their own development as individuals. The result is a continuance of parent-child relationships when in fact both parties should be moving towards the new arrangement of adult-adult relationships. Adolescence, arrested in its growth, benefits no one. When adolescent children refuse to grow up, the red flag should also go up for parents to examine their own behavior very closely.

The crucial obligation of parents is to teach their children how to be adults. During that process they may actually become fully independent adults themselves—free from parenting or unhealthy ties to their children. Parents have earned a break from the parenting responsibilities they assumed and have fulfilled to the best of their ability. Young people are capable of accepting increasing responsibility for themselves as they become adults.

Any normal person over eighteen is capable of becoming an adult. While we do not expect adulthood to be fully accomplished at eighteen, we hope that it will certainly be progressing rapidly. In the same vein, we would also hope that about four or five years later, adulthood will be fairly well established. If not, then the ground work has been laid in a person's life for conflict in relationship and living.

Gradually increasing responsibility encourages the development of self-esteem, a vital ingredient in the recipe for adulthood. Our experiences, both personally and professionally, have convinced us we owe it to young people to lead them through the complex process psychologists call separation-individuation. This process enables them to become independent adults and is discussed in detail in Chapter Two.

Independence and Rebellion

In the process of becoming an independent adult, a certain amount of rebellion accompanies the transition to adulthood. Examples of rebellious behavior which can be viewed **in the long run** as healthy declarations of independence include: staying out all night, brief experimentation with "forbidden" sex, alcohol or drugs, verbally deriding parental values, mischief which annoys the "establishment," and unusual clothing and hair styles. A distinction needs to be made, however, between rebellion leading to adult independence and rebellious adolescent behavior leading to a continuation of difficulties. The latter is often characterized by dramatic and even destructive examples of behavior, such as criminal behavior, alcohol or drug abuse, suicide threats, unsanitary personal hygiene which goes beyond such idiosyncrasies as unusual hair or clothing, and support of radical exploitive causes having nothing to do with one's own life.

Adolescents often take a contrary position on **any** issue merely to assert their ability to do so, or to act out their frustrations. While a certain amount of rebellion is necessary, unfortunately, many so-called "independent" adults are simply halted at the stage of adolescent rebellion. Their protests and rebellion continue and their declaration of independence remains incomplete. We all know those who will pout, sulk, and become obstinate and contrary when their whims aren't satisfied. To make the transition to adulthood means going beyond the fear of separating from those they have depended upon and beyond doubt in themselves. It means going beyond feelings of being rejected and the need to reject others or punish them through dramatized and destructive protest and rebellion.

Giving Up Old Roles

An old Jewish rabbi aptly said that the best parents are the ones who work their way out of the job. Parents need to experience an end to the responsibility of parenting when their offspring are able to assume adult responsibility for themselves. Adolescents deserve a break from being treated as children. Middle aged singles and couples need adult independence to live fulfilled lives on their own. Older parents have earned their freedom from child-rearing responsibilities.

In dependent relationships, one or both parties can't meet their own necessities and needs. Frequently they can't even admit their weaknesses to themselves and they defend against anyone knowing their fears. In independent relationships, both parties know the other person can live without them, even though they may still choose to rely upon each other for support which complements their own strengths or weaknesses. Obviously that can not be the case between young children and parents, but it certainly can be the relationship between mutually independent adults. Adults can acknowledge their shortcomings and needs to each other and consciously act to help themselves and one another.

The unhealthy protraction of the parent-child relationship doesn't pertain to only those from about 18 to 25. The case of Ruth, age 70, is an example that is occurring with increasing frequency. Ruth came for counseling in an acute state of fear and exhaustion. She had been awake for three nights worrying about her 39 year old, unmarried daughter who lived about 1200 miles away. During the many late night telephone calls to her mother, the daughter had disclosed her state of depression, ideas about suicide, drug and alcohol abuse, and details of her painful relationship with a thrice divorced, womanizing, unfaithful, drug-dealing boy friend.

Ruth felt the burning need to rescue her daughter from these tribulations. Her guilt was overwhelming. Further discussion revealed that Ruth had always felt a special need to

care for and protect her daughter who had had a particularly
difficult time health-wise as a baby. Since the family was
financially well-to-do, Ruth had provided her daughter with the
best of everything. As a result of this arrangement, both mother
and daughter had such a close dependency bond that Ruth
admitted, "When my daughter is happy, I'm happy."

Over the years Ruth assumed responsibility for her
daughter's problems, and the daughter dutifully called her
mother every time she had one. Lately, though, Ruth was
frightened for her daughter and knew the situation was more
than she could handle alone. With help, Ruth, an intelligent
and perceptive woman, came to appreciate the necessity to
break up the parent-child relationship with her daughter. Assuming the role of adult, Ruth told her daughter that because
the problems were beyond Ruth's expertise, she should seek
psychotherapy.

Ruth withdrew financial support and insisted that her
daughter use her own considerable resources to help herself.
Subsequently, the daughter started individual and group therapy.
During occasional visits, Ruth also participated in a number of
therapy sessions with her daughter. Gradually mother and
daughter assumed adult roles with each other. It took each of
them time to work through the guilt and fear, but they did. Ruth
discovered that she could be happy even when her daughter was
not. Both the mother and daughter in this case illustrate that
age is no barrier to dependent relationships and the parent is
just as susceptible as a grown child. In essence, both mother
and daughter were dependent upon each other.

Troubling Trends

Across the country more and more people are suspecting
that something is wrong with a system that requires life-time
obligations in raising children and then caring for elderly
parents. It's time for everyone to put away the guilt associated
with the growing number of obligations for adolescent and
grown children. It's time for the elderly to face the fact that in

American society the old-fashioned extended family is disappearing or is no longer necessary. The elderly no longer need to depend on their grown children to take care of them, and alternatively, their grown children have no right to impose upon older parents for support throughout their lives.

The children of this generation, who have had the greatest material advantages in history, are in trouble. Drug and alcohol abuse is rampant, and the psychological drain on guilt-ridden parents and addicted young people is appalling. The divorce rate is about 50%. Unplanned and unwanted pregnancies are increasing. An estimated 3 to 4 million American grandmothers and great-grandmothers have primary-care responsibility for their grandchildren, a figure which is almost certainly understated.

For the past few decades, women have been speaking out with rage about their own dependency on bullying husbands and bosses who, they claim, have exploited them. Men are questioning whether success in the workplace may have come at the expense of deeper or more honest relationships, especially at home. Teenagers today are turning to drugs, dropping out, and committing suicide at a rate that has world observers wondering about the future of affluent America. For approximately a decade, Americans between the ages of 16 and 24 have been the only sector of the population whose death rate has increased. Older parents are desperately trying to save their limited money and free time from the endless demands of grown children who are unable to support themselves. And it's all too easy to point the finger of blame at someone else.

Parents have literally mortgaged their future to provide for what they think are educational advantages for often ungrateful or irresponsible children. These may include paying to keep them in college, graduate, medical or law schools until they are in their thirties or older. Or it may mean financing their first automobiles or home mortgages, because they simply must start out with cars and homes at a certain "standard of living," or welcoming them with open arms to return to the home nest when they lose their jobs or spouses.

But the alarm sounds when we read the report released in the spring of 1990 which was commissioned by the National Association of State Boards of Education and the American Medical Association. Bluntly stated, today's teenagers "are unlikely to attain the high levels of education achievement required for success in the 21st century." The report cites drinking, drugs, unplanned pregnancies, violence, suicide, venereal disease, and emotional problems as some of the contributing factors.

Evidence is piling up that concern for the health of the next generation of adults is not unfounded. Young people in America today are taking their time about reaching adulthood. Many never do. And why not? Commitments to schooling, jobs, or relationships can be put on hold or dissolved quite easily as long as parents are willing to stand by, foot the bills, and welcome the uncommitted person back into the nest.

Increasingly we are seeing dilemmas such as an elderly couple experiencing frustration when a son or daughter announces divorce. The grown children move back home when their marriages fall apart. Without anyone even noticing how it happens, they all slip back into their old ways of behaving toward each other. Parents re-assume financial responsibility for everyone living at home. Subtle expectations are placed upon the grown children to account for their actions, to help more around the house, to show a little appreciation.

And in far too many cases, the parents harbor resentment, especially when they find their short-lived freedom curtailed by responsibilities for the grandchildren as well. Their grown children are indignant, because they feel their parents don't understand, or they aren't helping more graciously, or they really don't care enough. In this example, we see parents, and we see children, but we don't see independent adults. In these situations, no one has truly grown up completely.

Our objective is to help anyone at any age to understand and face the fears that prevent them or any other family member from growing up completely. Growth is the reward for those determined to work through unresolved immature tendencies.

Marketing Dependency

In a society where advertising and television constantly create unrealistic expectations, people must on occasion disagree with the media where obligations to children and elderly parents are concerned. Just because our society is more affluent than ever before, we need to beware of the subliminal, and sometimes overt, forces that will try to persuade everyone to spend their disposable resources to help able family members. It may only keep them dependent longer.

Recently, a bank ran a series of advertisements on local television which, for us, epitomized subliminal influence. In one particular commercial, an elderly couple was sitting in a comfortable living room when the telephone rang. The father answered, and we heard his responses to a conversation with one of his married children.

How happy the father in this television commercial was that the young couple had found their dream home. Unfortunately, they were having difficulty coming up with the down payment. The father hung up the phone, turned to his eager wife, explained the situation and said, "Guess I'll have to go to the bank tomorrow." To which his wife said, "Isn't that what parents are for?" End of commercial.

The next day we called the president of the bank and told him that putting the down payment on their children's first home is not what we thought parents were for. We told him we resented an advertisement that plants such ideas and tried to explain about the guilt and sense of entitlement generated by that kind of thinking.

The bank president, who was obviously pleased with the newly identified market for more loans, argued that we didn't want to help our children. We tried to explain the difference between help that encourages independent living, and help that is fear or guilt-based and leads to dependency. We may not have succeeded in changing his mind with a ten minute telephone conversation, but we know that particular advertisement was not aired again. He may have had other calls as well.

Even if people have unconsciously bought into the idea that families will not love them if they don't give them what they want, the families themselves need not suffer those consequences for the rest of their lives. They can begin to change. Parents do not "own" their children; nor can they buy their love and affection. Moreover, trying to do so frequently breeds resentment in the children, as many affluent parents discover when children who are given everything show little or no gratitude, run away or leave home never to return in any meaningful way again.

A Radical Approach

Many readers will be disturbed because we encourage people to be firm in their commitment not to supply all the physical and psychological demands made upon them by other able people. We are confident in the abilities of people to progressively satisfy their own desires and needs. We are not saying that we never give others help and support, but rather we only give what they cannot reasonably get for themselves.

People should be allowed generally to experience the consequences of their own behavior, even if it is negative. Help is freely offered when necessary, and withheld when detrimental to growth. To do otherwise would reinforce dependency and deny everyone the opportunity to learn.

Granted our approach to parenting may seem radical to some; it may even mean going against current trends. Our existing socio-economic system pressures parents into silently bearing the burdens of their offsprings' protracted adolescence, even when the children are in their twenties or older. Few dare buck the system. After all, if we don't support our children and their frequently expensive "necessities," we are "bad" parents. And our children will suffer their entire lives because of our selfishness. Right? We say, wrong!

In fact, we advocate the same approach to dealing with capable elderly individuals who have regressed into immature behavior as we do with young people who are in the process of becoming adults. They may have to back up in order to grow up into fully functioning adults. They, too, need to experience the freedom and self-confidence that comes from "response-able" independent living. What they do not need is parenting from their grown children.

Perhaps at this point it has become obvious that we place adult independence very high on the list of necessary human achievements. We often do this at the expense of "established" values. The "sacred cows" of marriage, the family, the home-town, college, standard of living, a particular job or house are sincerely questioned throughout the book. For example, when we refer to the "sacred cow" of marriage, what we mean is the marriage that was never a marriage in the first place does not have to continue at all costs. The "sanctity" of such a marriage might have to be annulled. If passion, intimacy, and commit-ment were never really present in the marriage to begin with, and they are not there now, then why go on with the charade?

People in marriages characterized by assault, adultery, addiction, and abandonment do not have to stay in the mar-riage—they can separate. Granted, some people can save such marriages by trying to start over and by seeking help in the process, but when the marriage still does not work, it can't be helped. It is likely that the children of such a "marriage" would be better off without it, too, because children who don't see love have difficulty learning love or may even think love is impossible.

The family that must stay together under any circum-stance is also questioned. When a family is dysfunctional or becomes a prison of mental or physical violence, the people involved are better separated from each other for the benefit of all concerned. Perhaps they can come back together at a later time after objective help has been sought and obtained, but perhaps they would be better off remaining separated and working towards forgiving and letting each other go.

Being raised to believe "my family, right or wrong, my family" teaches unfairness. The child who sees his mother unjustly attacking the neighbor lady or one of the elementary school teachers and is told when he brings it to his mother's attention, "You always stick by your family," has learned unfairness. It is true that families are the basis of society, but it is also true that dysfunctional, unfair families are the basis of dysfunctional, unfair societies. It is better to dissolve such a family or allow it to be absorbed into the larger community such as foster homes, foster parents, communal living, or extended families, than it is to have such a family continue at all costs.

The "sacred cow" of college for everyone is discussed in detail in Chapter Four. Sufficient for now, we will merely say that colleges are not for everyone and they can actually delay or impede growth toward adult independence, especially when the college is just a "holding tank" or "babysitter."

Having to find or to keep a job in one's special or particular field is another questionable "sacred cow." If skills are no longer needed in a particular field and there is no work available, then why must so many individuals go on doing nothing, collecting checks, or waiting for the government, an employer, or the union to "create" some meaningless, unproductive work for them? The situation is detrimental to a person's self-esteem and to the economy. Individuals in these circumstances are better off finding a new field of work, learning new skills, and going on with productive lives even if they have to accept reduced salaries, work in new geographic areas, or start their own business. The effort is worth the self-respect and productivity gained.

Also, who ever said that the house or home people live in must be the one in which they have to live out their days and that no other will do? We don't know who said it, but we don't think it makes sense. Many people in the last decade bought a home and have mortgages that are over their heads and that they can no longer afford. The situation breeds continual pressure and frustration. We think it makes more sense to sell, even at a loss, and find another less expensive housing option. The home then loses its function as a financial and psychological prison and becomes a meaningful asset, rather than a crippling liability.

The day is rapidly approaching, and in many places throughout the globe the day has already arrived, when the availability of the fenced-in single family dwelling is replaced by centralized apartments and condominiums. For many, uprooting and leaving behind the memories of a painful or security-bound past associated with a particular house is the first step to embarking upon a new life of independence. No, we are not referring to the plight of the homeless, but the able homebound—there is a difference. The question of how long someone else's home is "yours to call home" is an issue discussed in detail in Chapter Three.

Also up for "sacred cow" consideration is the notion that the geographic location where people grow up or where they are now working and living is the only one acceptable to them. Would that we could be as flexible as the native Americans who moved from place to place according to the abundance of game, water, or the fertility of the soil. For some reason, though, many people today feel they have an inalienable right to live in one fixed place. But if housing costs are prohibitive and there are no jobs in the area, they can move to another area rather than act helpless, complain, and get down on themselves or society in general.

During the last few decades people have assumed that their standard of living "should" steadily rise or at worst remain fixed. Most people shudder with horror at having to accept less and many would rather continue to make themselves miserable in jobs that are dedicated to the pursuit of more goods and services. Fortunately most Americans have a standard of living where a fixed or even lesser standard of living would still be quite comfortable. We emphasize that if people incorporate independence, happiness, and freedom into their standard of living and then go for what they want out of life, not only will they be more content, but they will also experience a wealth that goes beyond material goods and services.

Comparisons with Co-Dependency

Recently, co-dependency literature and programs have become so popular and available that something resembling a national movement is occurring. Since such is the case, it is appropriate before we conclude this chapter to point out several differences between the approach in **On Your Own** and most co-dependency literature or programs.

First, co-dependency literature and programs usually emphasize the necessity to identify and to work through childhood trauma and the early effects of dysfunctional families. **On Your Own** accepts the necessity to do so for those who have been traumatized or who come from such families, but we posit that the majority of dependency difficulties stems from the failure to further individuate from the age of approximately eighteen years onward. People suffering from these dependency difficulties were not necessarily abused as children, nor did they come from dysfunctional families. Rather, most dependent people were developmentally arrested at late adolescence. Arrested and protracted adolescence is the focus of **On Your Own**. We shift the emphasis from going back to childhood and working through traumas, although for some people this approach may also be necessary, and emphasize the necessity to begin right now to act, think, feel, and be on your own.

Second, the co-dependency approach to recovery usually advocates working a Twelve Step Program similar to Alcoholics, Narcotics, Gamblers, Overeaters, Sex Abusers Anonymous, and Anon. The program is considered lifetime in nature and also includes extensive involvement with a support group. **On Your Own** recognizes that for many this may be necessary, but for the majority of dependent people such a program or group is not required or is only needed temporarily. We see growth itself as a lifetime program that proceeds from stage to stage. Having to stay arrested at a particular stage such as the adolescent ego/emotional stage is not necessarily viewed as a life-time impediment.

Third, for recovery to take place following the co-dependency approach, people must admit they are powerless over the problem and that they need to turn their will and lives over to the higher power. Again, while **On Your Own** accepts this as the ultimate necessity, it emphasizes more the proximate and practical necessity for people to declare their independence, become emotionally mature, establish and strengthen their egos or self-concepts, face their fears, and go out to get what they want when it doesn't come their way. They do not wait for the higher power to do for them what they can do for themselves right now.

People have the power (or if preferred, they are the power) and can take responsibility for themselves in their own hands. After they have established themselves in this way, they can go beyond themselves to the higher power however it is defined. Further discussion on the subject appears in Chapter Six, Adulthood and the Expansion of Awareness.

This, then, is the basis from which we write **On Your Own**. We want you to realize this is not just another book on co-dependency or techniques for improving communications and hence relationships. We acknowledge the importance of good, healthy, open lines of communication, but we intend to go further than that. We intend to protect adult needs such as the needs for personal and economic independence and freedom from what is too rapidly in America becoming the never-ending obligations to able-bodied citizens ages 18 to 100.

The sooner all individuals gain awareness of the factors contributing to the process we call healthy separation-individuation (defined in detail in Chapter Two) the sooner they can begin to practice the actions necessary to ensure the transition from childhood to adulthood. We can help readers determine ways to encourage the natural growth process on every level of life, for their children, their elderly parents, and especially for themselves. If in the process of helping others grow up, people discover areas within themselves where growth is incomplete or has been arrested, another challenge presents itself: grow together and enjoy the most complete relationships possible.

There is no magic here; there is only determined action that comes from knowledge of the processes of growth and development that shape lives.

Chapter Two
Building Blocks and Stumbling Blocks

Chapter Two provides a framework for independence and for understanding the key concept of "separation-individuation" in six major areas of growth: physical, intellectual, social, moral, financial/vocational, and, especially, ego/emotional. This chapter explains how the basis for growth and development toward adulthood is laid down in childhood and adolescence. Particular emphasis is placed on the necessity for parent-child relationships to become adult-adult relationships. Personality disorders resulting from a failure to individuate are examined. Many real-life examples scattered throughout the chapter make it easy for readers to identify problem areas within their own lives and relationships. Some advice along the way to independence is offered.

In primitive societies, rites of passage from adolescence to adulthood were often marked by accomplishing certain dangerous tasks or participating in highly ritualistic ceremonies. Perhaps it was going out to kill a wild animal, living alone in the forest, or a young woman having a baby. These events were clearly defined, and the participants thereafter were given adult rewards and responsibilities.

Compared to primitive societies, the transition from childhood to adulthood is considerably drawn out in modern Western society. The age cannot be so easily defined and, in America, even varies from state to state. It is often confused by inconsistencies, such as the age for being drafted (18), or quitting school and working full-time (16), voting (18), driving a car (16), drinking alcoholic beverages (21), committing adult crimes (17), or marrying (18). Too often adolescence just goes on and on. Consequently, people may suffer from problems related to identity and immature relationships.

Because young people are taking their time reaching adulthood, they marry later, though the legal age for marriage in most states, and, implicitly, parenthood is 18 . The average age for males is 25 and females 23 and rising. They take more time to complete college and are generally discouraged from early entry into the labor force or marriage. It is not uncommon to drop out of college and do nothing for at least a year.

More and more people live on and off with their parents whether or not they go to college, and not merely for economic reasons. The parents' homes have become as much emotional havens as they are economic backstops. These are just some of the signs that separation from parents is taking longer. When independence does not begin early in childhood or continue throughout adolescence, it leads to dependency that extends into middle and old age.

If we are going to stop the trend toward protracted child-adolescence and prolonged parenting, the first and most important step is to understand the process a person goes through to become an adult. The process or transformation which takes place within as people grow and become independent adults can be called separation-individuation. During this process a person needs to master some specific developmental tasks within a variety of areas. Since a person can get "hung up" within one or more of these different areas, we can appreciate the variety of complications that can arise as personalities take shape or get stuck along the way.

There are six major areas where it is necessary to become independent in order to move to adulthood: physical, intellectual, social, moral/ethical, vocational/financial, and ego/emotional. Growing up happens gradually, encompassing a range of tasks within each of these major areas. As older adolescents move into adulthood, more and more evidence of independence in these major areas can be seen. The increasing independence is the surest signal to parents that older adolescents deserve increasing recognition as adults and more opportunities to demonstrate further maturity and competence.

Experience an arrest in one area, and people may still be treated superficially as adults by society, but deep within, that deficiency or incomplete growth will cause periodic havoc in their lives, and the lives of those around them. If growth in any of these areas is incomplete, the growth must occur at a later age. If it does not occur at a later age, the person is unable to live a complete and fulfilled life as an adult.

Physical Independence
("The outward signs of maturity")

What does it mean to be physically independent? At first glance we mean that individuals are capable of caring for their own basic physical needs in life, such as food, clothing, and development of motor skills needed for handling their own affairs. On an advanced physiological level, an adult is responsible for maintaining health, well-being, and physical development.

Sexual maturation and independence typically have wide social, moral, and psychological ramifications. From a

physical point of view, we would expect that young people
about eighteen years old will have achieved sexual maturation.
All the basic parts are in place and capable of functioning
normally.

Being sexually independent, though, involves much more
than just being able to function sexually. It involves being
responsible for one's sexual behavior. If the young person is
sexually active, is he or she practicing safe sex? Not to do so
today can result in tragedy. Practicing safe sex is an adult
behavior. With the knowledge available today, unwanted
pregnancies, venereal disease, and AIDS are not the results of
adult sexual independence. Quite the contrary, they are due to
the lack of it. Sexual freedom and independence go hand in
hand with responsibility. Having the freedom to choose to
engage in sex activity implies responsibility for the results of
the actions.

We are all familiar with young people's obsession with
their changing or changed bodies. Often the target of countless
jokes, the pain that adolescents endure because of the physical
changes can be significant. Hair, clothing, voice, make-up,
physique, diet, and exercise become all important. The physically mature body has finally completed the obvious changes
of puberty and assumed sexual maturation.

More often than not, parents have difficulty accepting or
are frightened by the physical maturity of their daughters or
sons. They realize these adult bodies are capable of reproduc-
tion. Surveys indicate the majority of young people are already
engaging in sex before they leave their teens. Are we naive to
think we can stop them? But parents fear, because they know
these adult-like bodies are ill-prepared emotionally for the
responsibilities of relationships and parenting. Ultimately,
physical independence is marked by responsibility for one's
own physical and sexual functioning, limitations, needs, and
behavior.

Physical independence also assumes that a person is
responsible for a routine of fairly regular meals, sleep, and

exercise. We do not think it is the job of parents to tell college-age people what to eat or when to get out of bed in the morning, even if it means they miss meals or appointments. In a truly adult state, physical maturation has evolved from early childhood dependence on the parents for all physical needs to physical independence in every way: they can feed, clothe, shelter, and maintain a routine of rest and activity without the assistance or interference of parents.

One woman, a widow and mother of three college-age sons, was at her wit's end because of her third son. During his last years in high school, he developed a pattern of not getting up in the morning early enough to get to classes on time. The mother, who herself worked, had an elaborate alarm and wake-up system for him and was even known to rush home from work mid-morning when her son failed to get up or respond to telephone reminders. Needless to say, this caused problems at school, failure of courses, and tremendous strain at home.

Not until the mother was able to let go of the guilt associated with her inability to be at home when her son left for school was she able to see that there was no physical reason her son could not be responsible for his own sleeping habits and commitments. Yes, it required her letting go of her need to "mother" him by wakening him in the morning. Also she had to stand by during the difficult transition period when her son nearly failed school until he was able to awaken himself in time. But the young man overcame his dependency. In the process, he took an important step forward in developing maturity and responsibility for himself. And so did his mother.

We are sharply aware that this phenomena of irresponsibility and immaturity exists not only with young people, but with the middle aged and elderly as well. We can recall the case of 71 year-old Mildred in Chapter One. She refused to feed herself. Our position on physical independence is that both the freedom and responsibility lie with the person and not with the parents or caregivers.

Harsh as it may sound, this same principle applies to the capable elderly. They need to do as much for themselves physically as they can. When people stop laying guilt on themselves or on their children, they can give each other what they really need—freedom **and** responsibility which leads to independence. If they do not start now, when will they? If they do not start now, the problems will go on and on and on...

Intellectual Independence
("That Doesn't Make Sense")

Being able to use the intellect or the discriminating faculty to reason and reach conclusions without depending upon outside help is intellectual independence. Others may contribute their ideas and opinions during that process, but the ability to discriminate on one's own is intellectual independence.

In the intellectual area, maturing adolescents enjoy the increasing ability to use logic and reason abstractly. The famous Swiss psychologist, Piaget, recognized this ability as beginning at approximately age 11. They now have ideas about ideas. Year by year, they are more capable of imagining their own future, and can figure out what will happen if they take, or do not take, certain actions. The shift to more abstract thinking leads to a creative, adult appreciation for symbolism, humor that may include sarcasm, irony and wit, and radical but reasonable conclusions about morality, religion, science, and philosophy.

Because adolescents who are maturing intellectually are thinking differently, they may see the world in a new way. They may become very critical of the world they are inheriting from their parents. They may be very observant of the slightest inconsistencies in rules around the house. They may even start confronting their parents on illogical behaviors.

Suddenly it may become obvious to older adolescents that their parents' habits (like excessive smoking, drinking, and burning the candle at both ends) conflict with the health rules that have been set for them (like what to eat and drink and when to go to bed). Parents may challenge these budding intellectuals, and then become infuriated when their own reasoning does not stand up to scrutiny.

The difficulty increases when neither accepts each other as they are, nor understands the changes that are happening, but each has a string of "shoulds" about the way the other person "ought" to think or act. What we mean by intellectual independence is not only to be able to think logically and abstractly, but also to be able to rationally validate assumptions, values, and preferences. And yes, these preferences might be quite different from ours or our parents. That, we believe, is the nature of independence!

The young, the middle aged, and the elderly all have their own assumptions, values, and preferences. If they can rationally validate those assumptions and preferences, then they are intellectually independent. In this sense, the intellect is used to evaluate, discriminate, and validate whatever it is that is valued.

In this way, we can see that the vast majority of the population is capable of intellectual independence. The obvious exceptions are pre-pubescent children, the retarded, neurologically impaired, and the disabled elderly. We need to understand that education and cognitive rehabilitation can and does bring many of these people to the point of functional readiness to assume more responsibility for themselves.

Social Independence
("But I'll Be So Lonely")

A major task in becoming an adult socially is to establish skills that enable a person to adapt to families, relationships, communities, and cultures. Adults, on the social level, are likely to have a stable sense of competence. They are generally able to meet and get along with others. When social independence occurs, individuals are capable of making their own friends, joining a social or peer group if they want to, and adapting to the social environment in which they live.

Parents and educators spend a great deal of time teaching children good manners and acceptable social skills. But more often than we care to admit, people acquire socialization skills on the way to adulthood by successfully passing through a series of painful experiences. How damaging these painful experiences are can determine how effectively people learn to accept themselves and others socially.

For example, the embarrassment experienced because a person used the wrong utensil at a dinner party may be just as devastating as harassment from bullies. In both cases, a painful lesson in conformity and socialization has been learned. The fear experienced when we learn from these painful social lessons may far outweigh the value of the lessons. These fears can further keep a person from enjoying social independence.

The degree of social independence may have nothing to do with a person's chronological age, educational, or vocational accomplishments. Cynthia, a 30 year-old teacher with a master's degree, is a case in point. Although Cynthia had a steady job and earned more than $30,000 a year, she still lived at home with her mother. Cynthia had no friends, no dates, and no social life.

Initially, Cynthia came to counseling filled with fears about living on her own. She was convinced that financially she could not afford to move away from her mother. As Cynthia's story unfolded, it became apparent to her that her real problem was not financial, but rather social. When Cynthia had become pregnant at sixteen, her mother had insisted that she have the child, remain at home, and allow her to help raise the baby. As it turned out, Cynthia's mother took over the care of the baby and raised the granddaughter as if she were Cynthia's sister.

In effect, Cynthia and her daughter, now an adolescent, were children together and continued to relate to Cynthia's mother as the parent. Cynthia carried a deep sense of social inferiority and was convinced that she did not fit in with her peers and never would. To some extent, her social mannerisms were that of an adolescent—she blushed, giggled, and shied away from the opposite sex.

Her mother's continued parenting held Cynthia back from assuming responsibility for her own social life and responsibilities for her own daughter. If Cynthia had a different personality, these circumstances just as easily could have produced a very angry woman rather than an introvert who was reluctant to be socially independent. As it was, Cynthia's inability to individuate socially was directly related to her inability to separate from her mother as a parent and her daughter as a child.

Cynthia realized that she was trapped by her fear of making it on her own socially. Through understanding of the major areas of growth in the process of becoming an adult, and with relentless urging and encouragement, particularly socially, Cynthia was able to make the necessary break from her mother. She moved into her own apartment, made friends, joined an environmental group, and despite the lost time, began to function as an independent adult with a normal social life.

We want to be careful not to confuse social independence with social acceptance or social adjustment. When we have to give up our own values and preferences to be socially accepted, then that is not independence. It is quite possible to be socially independent, but not socially accepted. It is also quite possible that adjustment to a sick society (the history of this century can provide a number of examples) can be an indication of social pathology which is quite different from social independence or being "on your own."

Moral Development
("Watch Out! Here Comes the Judge")

The process of maturing morally usually involves the progression from mere obedience as a way to avoid punishment, to a belief in the Golden Rule, to the recognition of universal principles of morality and to a personal commitment to those values. This is by no means easy, nor is it the norm.

The psychologist Kohlberg has researched moral development extensively.

Since experience is often the most effective teacher, we have to learn when to stop insisting on our own ideas of right and wrong, and when to allow others to discover what they value for themselves. These values may be learned from parents, society, religion, and teachers from all walks of life.

Moral adults are characterized by a value-based sensitivity to themselves, others, and nature. The state of moral adulthood usually comes after a time when a person has been exploring opinions about religion, sexual values, death, war, environment, politics, and other "big" topics of life.

Our society reflects the moral and ethical standards of the individuals who comprise it. People cannot help but live the values they hold within. This no doubt accounts for the ethical crises so prevalent today in business, government, health care, the environment, and other areas of life. It also accounts for the many expressions of compassion, generosity, and unselfish behavior exhibited daily.

Young people may rebel against a morality which does not seem real or fair to them. They may painfully challenge their parents and their beliefs. They may search for their own set of values by which to live, or they may not search at all. But one thing is certain, coercion doesn't work in the long run.

For centuries exponents of organized religions or governments in numerous forms have succeeded in enforcing a variety of behaviors, ranging from sexual repression to political fanaticism, through the threat of eternal damnation, ex-communication, imprisonment, exile, or death. But the loss of individual freedom or psychological health can be sustained for only so long before the human spirit rebels against unreasonable repressive forces. The astonishing changes underway around the world underscore this truth.

Whatever difficult stage an adolescent is in, parents must simply accept that the most effective teaching is by example. Parents may first have to examine themselves and start changes there. We ask young people to say "no" to drugs, sex, even certain music, and to say "yes" to work, school, and church. How many parents **really** enjoy their jobs, schooling, and religion? How many parents, who criticize their adolescents' flamboyant behavior, take no drugs and never sneak off to engage in **any** forbidden behaviors? Contradictions abound, and it is possible that older adolescents would benefit more from honest discussions with their parents about the difficulties inherent in ethical decisions, than a continuation of the "do-as-I-say-not-as-I-do" philosophy. With growing intellectual and moral sensitivity, discrepancies aren't easily ignored or missed. It is not uncommon for adolescents undergoing a moral awakening to rebel against their parents' values, whether justified or not. Parents forget how critically they themselves observed the world they first inherited from the last generation.

People can go through life with a moral code which they follow but which they do not claim as their own. It might take a crisis in mid-life to reveal the lack of commitment to values or issues which only then take on meaning in a person's life. For example, a woman may espouse a certain position on abortion or adultery, but it isn't until she finds herself or someone she loves involved in an unwanted pregnancy or an affair that she is confronted with testing the reality of her values. In effect, her morality is coming of age.

We cannot assume that chronological age is the criterion for moral independence. A middle aged or elderly person can be arrested at an immature level of moral development. Sometimes this occurs when someone has adopted a moral code strictly through social, religious, or political indoctrination, rather than through a code of ethics based upon intellectual discrimination, understanding, and experience.

We remember when Paul, age 48, first came for therapy because he felt guilty and depressed. Paul was unable to function sexually with his wife. He was experiencing a compulsive need to confess his "impure" thoughts about other women, and he was tortured by uncomfortable sexual sensations in the pelvic area. A significant part of Paul's therapy involved growing up morally from his childish perception of his bodily sensations and sex as bad, dirty, and sinful, to a healthy and accepting attitude. The process was slow and painful, since his religious indoctrination at an early age had been by misguided and vigorous individuals. With the help of an understanding clergyman who cooperated in his intensive therapy, Paul began to let go of his misconceptions and became an independent adult morally.

Vocational/Financial Responsibility
("Why Can't I Have It All?")

Individuals, who are used to the security of parents and parent-substitutes who provide all their needs, often assume that these providers will continue the support as long as the need remains. Parents or spouses may have an entirely different view on that subject, along with what constitutes "need." Older parents who indulged their own children by providing excessive financial support to them over the years may expect "pay back time" after they themselves retire. These differing viewpoints result in difficulties.

Financial independence, closely tied to vocational competency and independence, comes when people assume responsibility for earning, spending, and saving their own money. That does not mean one can never accept financial help. But able and competent adults are not regularly dependent on others for their financial security. Neither do adult parents bind their children to them by making those children financially dependent upon them.

As many women well know, the reluctance to achieve financial independence can, in some cases, keep people in psychological bondage or dependency and prevent them from becoming fulfilled adults. More and more women are discovering that they no longer need to be financially dependent on men for support, particularly when that support translates into pressure to endure an unhealthy relationship.

Many elderly people are quite capable of learning and using new vocational skills. Those who do are usually pleased with their new found interests, and they develop new or renewed self-confidence. Financial security in old age is something we all need to plan for individually. No longer do we live in a society where the custom is to have many children who are expected to take care of their parents when they get too old to provide for themselves. The younger generation doesn't stop caring or stop helping the older generation when it is necessary, but it is no longer a given that they **must** care or help.

One wealthy man confided his frustration during counseling over his grown children's financial dependence. He pointed out that when his children were growing up everyone said how important it was for him to provide all the material advantages he could for them. For him that meant living in the best neighborhoods, going to the best private schools, providing the latest and the finest money could buy, and bailing them out financially and legally whenever they were in trouble.

With one son in a drug rehabilitation center, the other an unemployed college drop out living at home, and us telling him he needed to cut the cord and let them stand on their own two feet financially, he cried, "What the hell is it? When they were growing up, I was told to give them everything I could, and now I'm told I spoiled them." The question was a good one.

The best guideline we can give is to repeat what we said earlier. As parents or as grown children of capable but older parents, we avoid giving help for the things family members can provide for themselves, and we allow them to experience the consequences of their own behavior, even when it is negative. Those involved in alcohol or drug rehabilitation know that it is necessary to allow substance abusers to experience the results of their actions for successful rehabilitation to occur. And yes, that could mean jail or loss of credit or similar negative circumstances.

We know of one couple who came to us confused when they discovered that their 20 year-old daughter, a junior in college, intended to live with her boyfriend at school in order to save money. She planned to use funds her parents were giving her for room and board to support this venture. On the one hand, the parents were pleased that she was trying to find a more economic living arrangement and that she was honest with them about her intentions. But, on the other hand, they didn't think she was ready to live with a man. They felt a serious relationship would not only distract her from her studies, but become an emotional burden she was not yet ready to handle.

We advised them to be completely honest with the young couple about their disapproval of the intended living arrangements. We also advised them to acknowledge that they could not stop the couple from living together, if they were prepared to make the required commitments. In short, we encouraged them to see this living arrangement as a declaration of independence by the young couple, one that deserved to be acknowledged and accepted by the parents, even if they did not agree with it.

At the same time, we assured the parents that they were under no obligation to financially support values they themselves did not hold. In other words, if the daughter insisted on living with her boyfriend, they could withdraw the room and board money from being used in this way.

Both the daughter and the young man admitted that they were unprepared financially and vocationally to accept full responsibility for their lives as a couple. In this case, the parents then asserted their right to refuse to support the couple financially, if the couple chose to assert their complete independence in every other area and live together sharing bed, board, and their daily lives.

Instead of driving this family apart, the confrontation helped the young couple establish a more mature rapport with the parents. They began to discuss with the parents more realistic plans for the future, which included a plan to establish themselves financially and to temporarily hold off on living together until they could support themselves. Would they sleep together every chance they could? Probably. But the parents accepted that probability, even if they didn't agree with it. Nor could they control it.

Here are just a few more of the kinds of questions we think we ought to be asking ourselves as we encourage young people to accept more and more financial responsibility for themselves as adults. Are they helping to defray some of their tuition, room and board costs at college? Or if they are not in college and working, but still living at home, are they paying room and board? Who is buying their snacks, outside meals, and paying for their long distance calls?

Consider, also, the following financial questions. How young people look in clothing is very important to them, but are they at least beginning to buy some of their own clothes? Are they experimenting with providing their own housing, such as apartments and house-sharing during summer jobs? Are they even working at all? Have they even considered saving some money by staying in off-campus housing or finding someone who will share an apartment with them? It is interesting to note that many foreign universities do not provide dormitories and cafeterias. Many European parents assume no direct responsibility for providing these basics, but rather encourage their sons or daughters to live or work, perhaps even abroad, to support themselves in that effort.

We are not saying that we never help our children or others by giving them gifts or assistance. What we mean is that we don't make others, no matter how old they are chronologically, dependent in areas where they are capable of independence. We don't deny people the satisfaction that comes from providing for their own needs. Help is freely offered when necessary and withheld when detrimental to growth and self-esteem.

Ego/Emotional Independence

("You make me feel so bad (or good) about myself.")

Over the years in the practice of counseling and therapy and in our personal experience, we have found the most difficult transition to adulthood takes place on what we call the ego/emotional level. We use ego and emotional together because they exist at the subtlest level of the human personality, and they most often operate together.

The ego is the nucleus of thoughts people have developed over time about themselves. That ego or self-concept (thoughts individuals have about themselves) is comprised of what they and other people have been telling them about who they are. These thoughts form the basis of what they have come to believe as the truth about themselves. Egos that have individuated are seen in people who genuinely understand, accept, and trust themselves.

Emotions are the feeling component of the personality. Emotional independence is being responsible and in charge of one's own feelings—confident one can handle one's own emotions, whether good or bad. Failure to individuate on the ego/emotional level usually results in thoughts and behaviors characterized by fear, anger, guilt, and not feeling good about oneself. Incomplete ego/emotional individuation is seen in people with diminished self-confidence. They are fearful or unable to control, moderate, or even get through emotional dilemmas.

People who have not individuated lose their awareness because of extreme emotions. They get severely upset when things are not working out as they wish. They don't believe in their own ability to get through emotional difficulties. They perceive parents or parent substitutes (i.e., spouse, special interest groups, religious leaders or employers) who come into their lives as responsible for them and how they feel. If they feel good, whoever they are depending upon gets the credit; "I couldn't live without my husband, he is so good." If they don't feel good, someone else also gets the blame; "My life is hell because of that woman I married." Successful separation-individuation on the ego/emotional level is characterized by people with a learned confidence in their own ability to face both challenge and denial.

Ego/Emotional Growth in Childhood and Adolescence

Although a crucial and difficult phase of separation-individuation takes place on the ego/emotional level in older adolescents, in actuality, the entire process of individuation begins in early childhood. By studying the same individual over a long period of time, as well as by studying different individuals at the same time, developmental psychologists such as Hall, Piaget, Kohlberg, and Erikson have discovered patterns of growth that apply to all of us. These patterns indicate that growth is a continuous process and that it proceeds in orderly stages, but of course at different rates of speed for different individuals.

As the human child adapts to physical existence, he or she achieves greater physical, mental, emotional, and psychological independence from everyone, including the parents. For example, imagine children of one or two-years of age gradually beginning to accomplish such basic developmental tasks as walking. As youngsters experience success, the ego strengthens and confidence rises, encouraging these children to see themselves as separate and somewhat independent from the parents.

If the process of separation doesn't begin to take place successfully during the early stages of development, the building blocks for later separation-individuation are not put into place. Because of this weak foundation, future growth is more difficult.

Imagine again the child who is learning to walk. What if the parents are very critical of the child's attempts at walking and in the extreme case even ridicule or punish the child's attempts, calling him or her stupid or clumsy? Or what if the parents of this child simply are not around for the child as he or she attempts to walk? If the parents are too busy with their own lives and problems, it is possible that no one will be there to give the encouragement, support, and confidence the child needs to accomplish some basic developmental tasks. Now imagine overprotected children whose parents constantly remind them that they can't walk yet; or they can't walk without the parents' help; or walking is too dangerous, and they will hurt themselves if they fall down.

In all of these examples, the children will probably have difficulties in walking (or whatever the task may be, such as reading, socializing, or learning anything in particular). They are blocked early on from becoming independent. And in all likelihood, the pattern of ineffective parental responses is repeated over and over in hundreds of different ways. The best advice is to encourage children to be independent by communicating support and confidence and allowing them to help themselves whenever possible, starting as early as possible. **Discouraging independence at any age sends the same critical message: a vote of no confidence.**

If we examine these same parent-child relationships on the ego/emotional level, we will see similar impediments to separation-individuation. If the parents are too harsh or critical, children may fear separation on the ego/emotional level. They fear going it alone. If there are no parents around, children might avoid tasks that encourage independence. If the parents are overprotective, the opportunity for success may be lost and the necessary risks not taken. The whole process of independence may become too threatening when children are not getting the necessary opportunities, encouragement and support. Taking risks is simply too scary.

If a growing child or adolescent doesn't become separated in a gradual way from the parents, dependency can be transferred later on to other significant individuals in their lives. For example, people whose growth is arrested in the adolescent stage of development can transfer the condition into their marriage relationships. These individuals go into the marriage with the expectation that they will be taken care of by the spouse, just as they were by the parents. When they are not, they behave like frustrated children, throwing a tantrum, pouting, or sulking. At the basis of the frustration is the fear of being on their own. Every time they get into a situation that requires independence, they are threatened and feel the need to defend against resolving that conflict. How? Too often by manipulating the people involved into "parenting" their problems away.

Let's recall the example given when we were talking about financial/vocational independence and the couple who wanted to live together at school. The couple decided to postpone their plans to live together because they could not yet assume complete financial independence and provide their own room and board expenses. In exchange for the parent's continued financial assistance, they would complete their undergraduate degrees before making a complete commitment to each other and living on their own.

Equally important to the financial independence in this example is ego/emotional independence. In the past when the daughter didn't get what she wanted from her parents, she angrily rebelled against them and authority in general. The parents were unsure whether she was independent enough to really be involved in a serious relationship with a man. Their fear was that she would become dependent upon the young man before she had had an opportunity to actually become adult on the ego/emotional level for herself.

The daughter's mature reaction to the refusal to support her financially if she lived with this young man was substantial proof that she was indeed becoming more ego/emotionally independent. The daughter did not fall apart, throw a tantrum, or threaten to run away. She was disappointed, but sensible enough to agree with her boyfriend that they did not want to accept all the responsibilities for living on their own.

On the one hand, individuals unable to make critical separations doubt themselves and their own ability to live independently. On the other hand, they doubt the love of those upon whom they are dependent. The failure to separate leads to a sense of doubt about the very people upon whom one depends for love and support. "If you love me, you will take care of me and do what I want you to do," echoes in the deep, unconscious of the person who is testing others. This doubt leads to feelings of rejection, which leads to constantly setting up tests or situations to prove just how unloved the person really is.

Testing frequently happens when the spouse of an elderly parent dies. The surviving parent often regresses into dependency upon his or her grown children and challenges them to the limit. The response of the children could determine whether capable elderly parents will continue to live productive lives on their own or whether they will start the inevitable and steady decline to total dependency and even an early death.

The testing can go on until the caregivers are ultimately defeated or fail to prove unconditional love. We recall yet another example of an adolescent daughter of a wealthy couple who tried to give her anything she wanted. They failed the test at her high school graduation when they gave her a new Ford instead of a BMW!

Protracted adolescence that is taking the form of destructive rebelliousness can lead to futile dramas with a variety of scenes, such as running away from home, getting into drugs, quitting jobs, dropping out of school, or moving into "crash" pads with other angry people. The theme revolves around the never-resolved conflict between childish dependence and rebellious and destructive independence. But this situation is not always or entirely the fault of adolescents. Parents who refuse to allow their children to grow up gradually may be planting the seeds for excessive rebellion from their own excessive controlling and parenting.

Older parents who engage in excessive controlling behavior by constantly interfering in the lives of their grown children may be in for a shock. Their children could finally grow up despite their parents and assert themselves against their parents' unnecessary controlling behavior. Many older immature parents over react to their children's' independence by cutting them out of their lives. Their final punishment often takes the form of threatening to withhold an inheritance unless they behave as they are expected—that is, dependently.

How many people do you know who spend their entire lives within the limitations of dependence and destructive rebellion because they refuse to grow up? If the boss at the office says "black," they say "white." If they make a mistake, they never admit it, but will argue inexhaustibly for their position. Perhaps their parents, through their own ignorance, set up the ideal conditions for dependence, but it is up to them, at any time, at any age, to finally break out of that dependency. Many of their rebellious attitudes are screams for attention, which could be traced back to unresolved fears of abandonment by the parents.

Some parents and adolescents unconsciously continue the frustrating drama of protracted adolescence and constant bickering. They are not aware of the real dynamics of their relationships within themselves or with each other. Other parents have intuitively done what was appropriate in raising their children, so that separation-individuation occurs spontaneously. So let's go back to the simple example of the parents and the children learning to walk for some clues to the difference.

Some parents might find themselves with their arms outstretched to their children who are about to walk, saying things like, "Come on, you can do it; sure you can walk; it's OK." These parents communicate a sincere confidence in the children's abilities. With each success, they reinforce that confidence through realistic support. The children can even make mistakes, and in fact do make mistakes, without parents destroying their tender concepts of self. "Oops, that's OK, come on and try again." So the process leading to separation-individuation doesn't occur at a set point in time. It started back in childhood and gradually built up to the later stages where healthy independence can occur.

We can't go back and change what occurred fifteen or twenty years ago. But we can **understand** what happened. With that understanding we can become more **aware of why we behave the way we do.** Awareness, then, and understanding give us the **freedom to act differently.** Actions taken today can produce independence now and in the future.

Young children relate to their parents as rewarding or punishing objects. As children grow they relate less and less to parents and significant others as objects and more and more to them as persons. Children, and too many adolescents, have little consideration for their parents as human beings with feelings, needs, and even rights. For these children and adolescents, the parents are merely providers–that is, **objects** to be taken for granted–not adults who can be related to as equals.

How many children do you know who sit around and ponder the generosity of their parents as expressed by their latest gift, whether it's a new toy or the paid receipt for their college tuition? Adolescents seldom question their right to live at home and receive all their parents support until they are twenty-one and even beyond, regardless of whether they are going to school, working, or returning home because of a failed marriage.

Children and many adolescents simply don't think that way. The classic statement parents make is, "You don't appreciate anything we do for you." The fact is, it is unrealistic to expect much more than self-centered behavior from children. But for an adolescent to become an adult, the ability to appreciate the feelings of others needs to become their experience, and does, as they accomplish the task of separation-individuation.

An Extraordinary Transformation

Exactly how the adolescent changes into a young adult is nothing short of astonishing and involves the six major areas discussed, all affected by such outside forces as culture and time in history. Growth in these areas is interdependent or what is now called holistic. Everything is moving along at the same time, some areas faster than others.

Most developmental psychologists would agree that the overriding task of adolescence, no matter what culture they live in, is to pull together some sense of identity of themselves. In order to do this, they need to separate physically and psychologically from their parents. Both parents and adolescents who live through this period know how tumultuous and disturbing it can be.

When separation from parents begins and ties to family are weakened, and when no one understands the necessity and importance of the process, pain and/or confusion frequently occur. This happens because adolescents transfer their allegiance to peer groups, who introduce new ideas, mores, and manners, and who dictate to adolescents how to relate socially, psychologically, and sexually to each other. During what is known as the conformist stage of adolescent development, parents are forced to the sidelines while adolescents deal with peer pressures and acceptance.

Some authorities believe that adolescents need to identify completely with peer groups, because that's the only way they can satisfactorily see themselves as separate from their families. The break, then, amounts to their first step in the development of individual identity. It makes no difference that expectations and rewards of the peer group often produce more conformity than individuality. What matters to maturing adolescents is that they see themselves as separate from parents. Besides weakening family ties, this major shift in identification serves other important purposes. It gives adolescents intense experiences relating to their own generation—something they will have to be able to do for the rest of their lives anyway.

If all proceeds typically, researchers tell us, and most parents know from experience, adolescents move through a highly unstable stage, characterized by mood swings, preoccupation with self-image and group acceptance, impulsiveness, abstract idealism with its moralistic cliches, intense loyalty, disdain for hypocrisy, fascination with material things, and the effect these things have on their reputations. If this description fits many older people we know, remember that many supposed adults have never successfully or completely passed through the stage called adolescence, no matter how old they are chronologically.

A number of interesting studies demonstrate how older adolescents exaggerate the differences between their own attitudes and those of their parents, while their parents tend to minimize these differences. Because the actual differences fall between these two extremes, it's important that the generations keep talking (arguing?) even if it seems futile. This is a time when the emphasis on negotiation can help narrow the gap between those perceived differences, even when the conclusions rarely satisfy either generation completely.

But research across the life span also shows how this stage is gradually replaced by a more conscientious period. Status as a group member gives way to an awareness of personal goals, beliefs, and autonomy. Just as it was necessary for adolescents to weaken ties to their families, emerging adults step away from the group. They now claim their own personal perspective on life in general, but more importantly, they claim a personal perspective on themselves.

In essence, some measure of autonomous identity is now apparent in the young person. Because of this distance or objectivity, young adults more selectively evaluate others (including parents) and surrounding events. They may still be far removed from positions their parents take, but they have the ability and desire to expand their views on the world.

At this stage, they can even sort our legitimately their own actual shortcomings and live with them or resolve them. "OK, so I'm not a brain, but if I work hard I can make it through college." Or, "I guess I am not really so dumb (or ugly, or undesirable) as I thought." Or, "College isn't for me, but I love working with my hands." Or, "I know I have to get help with these bouts of anger." Or, "I'm not hanging out with people who are into alcohol (or drugs, or irresponsible sex) anymore."

Modern society hasn't exactly made it easy for young people to pass through the peer-dominated jumble of mixed experiences on the way from adolescence to adulthood. In fact, we send enough mixed messages to confound the most stable person, let alone someone trying to sort out an identity. The media poses adolescents as witty and cynical, as much smarter and cuter than wimpy adults. Adults are worthy only of scorn. Adolescents have plenty of money (rarely self-earned), are catered to by a wide range of communications media (movies, records, TV), and form the basis of a powerful and intimidating subculture in society.

Our educational institutions segregate students by age, provide few cross-age experiences, little contact with adults outside the family, and few chances to identify with any potential role models in the "real" world. It is any wonder young people are reluctant to leave this subculture and become assimilated into the adult culture which has segregated them for so long?

But adolescents can and do pass through this confused and confusing stage. What is most important at this time is that parents and adolescents really understand the process and its difficulties, on both sides. No matter how strained relations get, parents have a role to play as parents and as adults.

When adolescents are capable of relating to their parents as independent adults, then both are ready for roles that are more fully expanded. An important part of that parent role is not prolonging the process any more than is really necessary. Granted, the parenting role is diminishing more and more as maturity progresses. But just as it is important for parents to be available for their children when it is really necessary, they must let go when opportunities for independence arise.

Whether parents realize it or not, they are important role models (either good or bad) for their children. This is true even while the formation of identity prompts the young adult to break away from parental influences. After adolescents resolve their identity crisis, they experience an increasing sense of wholeness about themselves. Finally, they are able to stand back, even if it is years later, and see themselves more objectively in relation to others, and that includes parents.

Once adolescents become young adults, their values and norms can, and frequently do, reflect their parents' orientation, but usually with some innovative distinctions. If parents have been open and honest with themselves while their adolescent children became adults, they, too, have modified their own way of looking at the world and themselves. Parents have as much to gain in moving toward the role of independent adult as do grown children.

During this accelerated period of growth perceptive parents grasp the second chance to work through some adolescent challenges they may have left incomplete. Each generation has a lot to teach the other. Young adults may express their commitments in their own ways, but similarities between the generations are often beneath the surface differences. Those difficult discussions, as both sides negotiated their way through the period of adolescence, are far from a waste of time.

Parent-Child to Adult-Adult

One reason parents might not have laid the proper foundation for separation-individuation in their children is because they haven't achieved adulthood themselves. Anyone past the age of twenty-five is automatically expected to have passed from adolescence to adulthood. It's difficult to relate to others as adults when they may not have learned how to be adults themselves. How can they interact as adults with peers or families if they have not individuated in all the six major areas of development just discussed?

For this reason we ask readers to take a hard look at their own behavior in order to help themselves, their spouses or partners, their parents, and their own children. For example, parents may feel tremendous guilt because they think they are not good enough to their children. Because they feel guilty, they may have an overwhelming need to continue to "help" their children.

But generosity isn't so much at the heart of this need, as is the underlying fear of letting go of the parent-role themselves. They need the relationship because it makes them feel good about themselves. Or perhaps they continue to tolerate selfish and inconsiderate behavior in relationships because they are terrified of the possibility that the other person will abandon them and leave them on their own.

It is possible that some people are so locked into the practiced roles of parent or dependent spouse or partner that they are afraid to let go of the role. People suffering from this condition may never have known any other roles than those of being children and then parents. They may never have passed through the separation-individuation process themselves.

The time eventually comes when children leave home and establish their own nest. Much to their surprise, parents who have not experienced complete individuation themselves have no idea how to be adults with their spouses, let alone with the young people who themselves need to separate.

Later, many parents of grown children discover that they have little going for them in their marriages because they've rarely related to each other as independent adults. This leads to all kinds of confusion, mid-life crises, and, too often, divorces. Unfortunately, people can change partners, but the scripts or dynamics repeat until the people involved become adults in their own right.

Part of the process of becoming adult human beings involves understanding and responding to the kinds of ideas presented here. Even though parents may have been operating from an adult basis in specific relationships with other people they know, or even live or work with, they must also become adults in their relationships with their adolescent sons or daughters, their spouses, or their elderly parents. In this way, people can step into adulthood and experience the growth that can lead to an entirely new way of being with family and friends. All parties involved must make the transition from parent-child relationships to adult-adult relationships. What a fantastic adventure awaits those who are courageous enough to discover the cause of their own dependency and determined enough to change.

What Happens if Separation-Individuation Doesn't Occur?

When separation-individuation isn't accomplished, the personality is adversely affected. What can result is a personality disorder that might take many different forms. Briefly, we'll mention a few examples here. Keep in mind that while each of the personality patterns can become clinical and serious in nature, many people exhibit them to a lesser extent. The patterns also are frequently mixed and overlapping.

Sometimes we encounter a type of personality that seems incomplete or **borderline**. Someone with a borderline personality exhibits a pervasive pattern of instability regarding moods, interpersonal relationships, and self-image. Though mature in many ways, people with this predisposition are merely bordering on adulthood. Like emotional yo-yos, they vacillate from immature to mature responses.

Sadly enough, they can even be arrested in this uncomfortable borderline state for a lifetime, perpetually defending themselves against fears of abandonment and depression. People who frequently engage in impulsive drinking, rage, binge eating, sex, substance abuse, shoplifting, reckless driving, or excessive spending are often manifesting borderline defensive behaviors. Intensive and extensive psychotherapy is usually needed for borderline personalities. It includes much confrontation and working through of acceptance and trust issues with the therapist since they usually have never trusted another adult.

A borderline personality exists because somewhere in early childhood a developmental arrest occurred when separation-individuation did not happen. Because of this condition, borderline personalities engage in a life-long defense against understanding and accepting themselves as they are. Since they didn't experience understanding and acceptance from others in childhood, they don't experience it later in relation to themselves and others.

Dependent personality is another disorder. It is much like the dependency we have been talking about but taken to the extreme. It is characterized by marked submissive, indecisive, non-assertive behavior. In this case, individuals look to others to do almost everything for them, to make all the decisions, and to provide for their needs and desires. Dependent people volunteer to do things that are unpleasant or demeaning in order to get other people to like them. They feel uncomfortable or helpless when they are alone, and they will go to great lengths to avoid being alone. They are easily hurt by criticism or disapproval.

The confusion or need for excessive advice or reassurance from others is often painfully obvious for those who live or work with dependent personalities. People who answer, "Whatever you like." every time someone asks them what they want, are often sending signals of over-dependency by their indecisiveness and submission. Unfortunately, dependent personalities lend themselves to exploitation and are devastated when close relationships end. Dependent people have great difficulty initiating projects, or doing things on their own. They agree with others out of fear of rejection, criticism, or disapproval. In the end, they come to experience that most people will find it is easier to take care of them than deal with their ineptness or indecisiveness, which, of course, can prolong their agony for a lifetime.

Another personality disorder and one which is particularly frustrating to others is the **passive-aggressive** adolescent or older person who is unconsciously suppressing anger toward someone or something. Because passive-aggressive individuals do not know how to responsibly assert themselves, nor can they risk active involvement for fear of punishment, they passively punish others by pouting, sulking, becoming obstinate, contrary, or procrastinating to the point of even undermining their own lives.

Perhaps one recognizes passive-aggressive behavior in the student who persists in bringing home bad grades or getting into trouble with the law. What better way to punish parents who they are convinced don't really care about them anyway? They blame their parents as "responsible" for their lack of freedom. But they can't break away from their parents either. Instead, they stubbornly undermine or sabotage life and fight a desperate battle in their self-defeating attempts to spoil life at home.

We can, of course, move forward in time and see the passive-aggressive adolescent many years later engaging in sabotaging behavior on the job. Nothing is ever right, no one is competent, and the boss is always at fault. The company is bound to fail, the products aren't any good, and no one listens to them anyway, so why bother. If these people marry and have their own children, the drama continues with plenty of pouting, sulking, and refusing to cooperate while they raise their families. The stage is set for a number of show-downs when, later in life, they become obstinate and difficult retirees.

People with passive-aggressive tendencies can't easily express what is really happening to them. Perhaps the scene goes something like this, "Would you like to go on vacation with us this year?" Adolescent or aged mother-in-law answers: "Not really." At which point the parents or grown children try to convince them what a great time they are all going to have together, until they finally begin to lose patience with the blatant lack of enthusiasm.

Perhaps this scene might even go several steps further, with the parents confronting the adolescents or aged relatives over their negative attitude, only to find themselves facing individuals who are increasingly obstinate, argumentative, deliberately slow or forgetful, resentful or scornful of anyone in authority, to say the least. In other examples, they may destructively rebel by vigorously voicing opposite views and values or by engaging in self-punishing forbidden behaviors, such as indiscriminate sex, taking drugs, or disappearing. What they are really attempting is to passively punish others, although they are not aware of what they are doing.

On the other end of the spectrum of personality problems are individuals with ego-bound or **narcissistic** disorders. Often while growing up, some individuals get an over-abundance of positive or negative reinforcement which causes them to expect and need perfection in themselves. Subsequently, like Narcissus, they fall in love with their own reflections and they are able only to see themselves as perfect. Narcissistic people are so stuck to the perfect image they must reflect that they can't form a healthy relationship with anyone, including themselves.

Narcissistic people search until they find somebody else who also thinks they are perfect or wonderful. They choose a mate who mirrors that perfect image back to them. Fortunately for them (but really unfortunately), there are plenty of dependent people in the world who are more than willing to spend their lives reinforcing the needs of the narcissist, as long as that wonderful or perfect person fulfills their dependency needs.

More often than most of us suspect, the narcissistic male teams up in marriage with the "Cinderella" dependent female, or occasionally, the other way around. If they are lucky, they wind up in counseling before the relationship self-destructs or withers away into a non-communicative or abusive disaster. It is very difficult for each of them to see and accept themselves as they truly are. If ego-bound people are particularly clever at manipulating, they can rise to very successful positions in business and society. But beneath the surface bravado, there is a child-adolescent craving attention and acceptance because his or her ego is not sufficiently independent to stand on its own.

Narcissists have never accepted themselves for who they truly are—strong in some areas and not so strong in others. These pained egotists, who looked so good and confident to their peers and bosses during their rise in business or society, often reveal the destructive side of their personalities when their authority, wealth, fame, power, or beauty are threatened.

A case of a female narcissist is exemplified by Sara, an attractive 39 year-old woman. Sara would tell you how high her IQ was soon after you met, so you'd be sure to treat her with the special respect she expected and needed. She dressed suggestively on the job and came on sexually with men, though she was known to be merely a tease. Sara was competent in her line of work, but argumentative and envious of those who were a threat to her. She exploited those whom she thought she could manipulate to her advantage, usually those with less talent or less forceful personalities than hers. She spread gossip vindictively about those she disliked, and always reacted with rage to any criticism of herself.

Sara's whole life centered around herself and how she looked to others, both literally and figuratively. Married to an adoring and accommodating man, she had worked hard to secure her job. Although the bloom was beginning to fade on her appearance, she still felt entitled to a more prestigious position and she was prepared to put down anyone who got in her way.

For Sara, her life was good when she was being recognized, and miserable when she was not. She wanted to be liked and respected, and badly needed recognition in order to maintain her image of herself. She was willing to sacrifice good relations on the job for the possibility of gaining status and visibility. She was her own worst enemy because she created hard feelings among her fellow workers, but couldn't see her role in causing them. In the final analysis, she could never advance past a certain level because most people in authority could not trust her. Sara was not yet an adult.

When narcissists become parents without ever having become complete adults, they create for their children the same psychological environment which prevented their own separation-individuation when they were young. They may treat their families with the same disdain as they do subordinates on the job. They demonstrate a grandiose sense of importance and will ignore information which doesn't support their positions. An adolescent has no more chance of feeling accepted or challenging the narcissist's ideas than employees do. Better to tell him or her what he or she wants to hear. It's safer that way. Narcissists usually go on until their supply of fame, wealth, power and beauty runs out, and then they get depressed. Psychotherapy is recommended for the narcissist and it includes considerable reflection of their pain rather than their grandiosity.

Any of these personality disorders can lead to patterns we have observed in people who are indignant when the world doesn't give them what they think they want, need, and deserve. This is especially true because they assume they are entitled to have their desires provided for them, if not by their parents, then whoever took their parents' place such as their spouses, employers, the university or the government. When desires are frustrated, anger results. When anger is unexpressed or unresolved, people eventually become depressed. With understanding, it becomes evident that beneath depression, caused by "de-pressing" frustration or unfulfilled desires, is the deeper condition of fear—fear of being on one's own on any of the levels mentioned earlier, such as social, ego/emotional or even vocational/financial.

Personality disorders don't just happen overnight to people. They develop gradually as they are laid down in formative childhood or adolescent years. The irrational and self-downing ideas people have about themselves are reinforced over and over again as they grow up, often by parents with similar or complementary problems. They are unlikely to go away instantly. But people can redirect their attention into healthy expressions of their individuality when understanding and awareness are introduced into their lives. Understanding and awareness are the keys that unlock the whole person within each of us.

Blocks Along the Way

Recognition and admittance of the problem are the first steps to understanding who we are on the way to complete adulthood. Although this does not have to be a painful experience, it certainly could be painful depending on how deep the difficulty is. At the basis of that pain is fear on the part of the person who in fact is still a child-adolescent in one or more of the major areas of development.

Guilt is often at the center of many caregivers' inability to let go when others are capable of taking care of themselves. Similarly, at the basis of this guilt is the fear of failing, which may take the form of rebuking themselves for not having done enough. Or perhaps they fear they are pushing their children out of the nest too fast, or expecting too much from the elderly.

Because of guilt, people convince themselves that they must provide more and more for individuals who are quite capable. We are reminded here of a single mother whose daughter was away at college during her freshman year. Out of guilt the mother kept giving and giving—allowances, automobile, clothing, vacations—until the daughter herself revealed in therapy that she wished her mother would stop because it was holding her back.

Many other caregivers continue parenting in order to fulfill the need to be needed or to be looked up to as the beneficent provider. They not only assume this role for their children, but often expect their spouse, friends, or co-workers to need them in the same irreplaceable way. In all these cases, the person is satisfying his or her own needs and not the needs of the other people to become independent individuals themselves.

When people don't feel good about themselves, they are always looking for someone else to give them positive feedback and reaffirm their worth. How many times we have seen "empty nesters" fall into depression when their children finally break away **from them**? How many healthy individuals deteriorate rapidly when they retire because their lives no longer have any perceived purpose? When we do not value ourselves from within based upon acceptance of who we are, as we are, we open ourselves up to dependence on manipulation from outside influences in our search for personal worth.

People need to know what can happen when they decide it's time to encourage family members at any age to take the steps towards independence. Because threatened individuals who are still basically child-adolescents may rebel outright and accuse their parents, spouses, friends, or children of not caring or being supportive, it's important to proceed gradually, systematically, and consistently. Perhaps the persons whose growth is arrested or regressed at immature levels will accuse family or friends of abandonment just when they think their need the greatest. Then the guilt sets in for those who tried to help a loved one overcome those immature tendencies.

When doubt sets in, it is **not** the time for family or friends to reverse decisions, change directions or lose confidence in themselves or the person's ability to become a mature adult. For example, parents cannot be strong when their image of themselves as competent and nurturing parents depends solely on the feedback adolescents give them. When parents are judging themselves based upon the reactions of their children or family around them, rather than upon a sound understanding of the principles of development and maturation, then the parents and the adolescents are dependent on each other.

Because of this dependency upon each other, neither will know how to end the pathological relationship. When this occurs, we recommend that both parties get assistance from a psychologist or counselor who understands and can facilitate the necessary growth. All parties involved need to reach a point when they can accept and honestly say, "We are doing the best that we can, and that's all we can do, and its OK (even if it's not perfect), no matter how it turns out."

The time needs to come when we all make that final break in order to begin relating to each other as adults. Parents don't own their children and vice-versa. They never did own each other, and certainly neither has the right to bind themselves for a lifetime of obligation. But if parents refuse to let go of their adolescents and adolescents refuse to grow up, all parties are in for a lifetime of suffering and anguish.

Even if family members never see each other again, the psychological damage from relationships where separation-individuation has not occurred could torment or distort their entire lives. Adolescents and parents will repeat a pattern which locks them both into an emotional prison. No matter what the status of a parent's relationship with an adolescent, it is not too late to work through the process of separation-individuation.

The sooner parents and/or adolescents start to understand the process of separation-individuation, the better. If parents wait until their grown children are twenty-five or older, and perhaps already married themselves or living their own lives apart from parents, these disorders may still be operative. It will be more difficult for everyone involved to gain the realizations that will allow them to relate to each other on the level of adult-to-adult.

As we said before, the process of maturation is not solely determined by chronological age. The middle aged and elderly are frequently immersed in the same struggles. There is the possibility that immature elderly parents are unable to appreciate the personal growth and independence that has taken place in their own middle aged children. They may accuse their grown children of being cold and hard-hearted when they, elderly parents, irrationally demand unnecessary support in their old age.

Anyone who needs assistance to facilitate the process of separation-individuation can get knowledgeable and professional help from therapists or counselors skilled in maintaining the necessary objectivity. Remember, some of these patterns of behavior have been going on for a long time. Some of the personality traits are deeply impressed, but none of the obstacles need to be viewed as impossible to overcome. Everyone can benefit.

It takes courage to look at personal strengths and weaknesses and a great deal of understanding before individuals accept themselves, not as they "should" be, but as they really are. This is the only place where real growth can start. The mark of an adult is honesty, understanding, and acceptance of oneself.

We realize many may claim our ideas seem out of the ordinary, and indeed they are. Proponents of prolonged adolescence argue that a lengthy period before a person assumes adult tasks is necessary to work out sexual and vocational identities and a coherent philosophy of life. Readers may cite authoritative views from educators, developmental specialists, parenting guidebooks and the media who recommend that parents "care for" and "love their children no matter what." We do not entirely disagree, but we question the point at which "care for" and "love" become overprotection and possession that fosters dependency. We question, too, whether giving privileges without responsibility can ever really lead to independence.

It is too easy in an affluent society to remain adolescents for a lifetime. Even adolescents can figure out the rules of social convention and play the game of consumer and producer. Almost anyone can get a job, make some money, and survive. But to really become an adult is to declare your independence and think, act, and be on your own.

Chapter Three
Rolling Out or Rolling Up the Welcome Mat

No other symbol of successfully becoming an adult is more apt than leaving the nest. And no other symbol is more revealing than returning to the nest at whatever age people are unsure of themselves. Different lifestyles resulting in difficulties in a variety of situations concerning living at home or away from home are addressed. These include the college-aged, youthful and employed, unemployed, married, divorced, separated, and the elderly. Acceptance versus agreement, assertion, and effective ways of handling frustration and anger are presented. Chapter Three emphasizes when and why being in the parents' home, the home of substitute parents, or, in the case of the elderly, being in the home of their children is destructive to independence and healthy maturation.

When their son and daughter were both away at college,
like so many other parents, David and Martha eagerly awaited
the Christmas holiday so they could enjoy their company. As
it turned out, the holiday lasted five weeks because it included
the semester break. The arrival home was accompanied with
the usual holiday chaos that precedes Christmas in the family.
But what struck them as truly extraordinary was the observa-
tion that within days after arrival home, both college-age
students had regressed to habits of childhood.

Suddenly, shoes and clothing were strewn everywhere.
Rooms were disasters; music blasted throughout the house
inconsiderately at the oddest hours; and sleeping and eating
patterns were unpredictable, making planning impossible.
Surprised, David and Martha found themselves having to "discuss" unacceptable behavior with their own college-age
children, as if adolescents were unfamiliar and resistant to the
family routine or parents' personal needs.

They were dismayed because they thought they had already worked through most of the family differences involving
consideration. Or were they more acutely dismayed because
they had gotten used to the calm and order of their children's
absence, and resisted the disruption of the household? In any
case, the situation was rapidly deteriorating.

Before long they confronted the grown children regarding
the situation. David and Martha asked, finally, if their son and
daughter treated their roommates with the same lack of consideration. Surprisingly, they said, candidly, "No". In short, the
grown children too began to laugh when they became aware of
how quickly they had slipped back into childhood patterns of
behavior.

Many of the activities in question had been bones of
contention during the high school years. Incidentally, since
then the students have come to understand that those bones of
contention had more to do with rebelliously testing parents and
declaring independence than with whether shoes were picked
up or chores completed.

Like so many parents who have repeatedly told their children, "Don't ever forget that you always have a home here," David and Martha realized the time had come to qualify this statement. When David and Martha tried to explain their position and attitude regarding home, some very important pieces of the larger picture of development came together in a meaningful, personal way for all of them.

David and Martha began to appreciate how encouraging or allowing children to live at home could have implications for a lifetime, for the children as well as for themselves. The issue of anyone over 18, including parents over 65, who are living at home, is the focus of this chapter. Keep in mind, though, that "children" could mean anyone from 18 to 100.

Coping With Different Lifestyles

The whole question of how older children relate to their parents with regard to their parents' home, or what elderly parents expect regarding their grown children's homes, concretely illustrates whether the people involved are behaving toward each other on the level of parent-child or adult-adult. It also provides one of the most powerful opportunities for parents and children to move from parent-child relationships to adult-adult relationships.

More parents are coming to understand their own guilt or fear, either because they enjoyed or were devastated by the freedom of an empty nest, or even one less child at home. Of course parents still care for their children and they want them to visit, but more and more parents are getting in touch with the disparity and tension between their own lifestyles and that of their older children.

As parents get older they come to terms with their own bodily aches, pains, and preferences; the effects of pressure from their jobs; their desire for their own friends, interests, and hobbies; the difference between the entertainment they prefer and that of their children; their own need for regular rest and their own style of recreation; and often their renewed sexual interest in each other, especially when children are not around. All are enhanced by the freedom of parents to do as they please, when they please, where they please in their own homes, sans the presence of grown children.

But the crux of the dilemma in so many homes today involves parents who have no difficulty recognizing the differences in their lifestyles, but who feel compelled to tolerate disagreeable conditions in their own lives because grown children live at home or return home for extended visits. The parents have convinced themselves that "good parents" tolerate extraordinary demands regarding children in the home because if they don't, they are not "giving" or "understanding" parents. Parents torture themselves with thoughts that their children might hate them, run away, or simply never visit, unless allowed to do as they please. Hence, guilt and fear.

People became parents because they either decided to have children or they finally accepted the children already in their lives. They didn't choose the particular personalities of the children they got. Neither did the children choose their parents' personalities. Ultimately, they got the children they deserved and needed, and the children got the parents they deserved and needed. All is well and wisely put, even if they don't understand at all times why they have to work through their differences.

When the values and lifestyles of parents and young people are incompatible, they either work out conflicting situations, or it's time to part ways. Difficult as it may sound, in some families parting is inevitable, and sometimes advisable. Often uncomfortable, sometimes painful, parting with children is still one of the most significant opportunities for growth for all parties concerned. And separation need not be permanent, although sometimes it is.

Parents can learn how to accept themselves—as they are—and to assert themselves as adults. That doesn't mean whining and complaining about how inconsiderate, spoiled, and demanding children are around the house; nor does it mean nagging and badgering ("guilt-tripping") about how self-sacrificing, helpful, and indispensable parents are. Acceptance doesn't necessarily mean agreement; acceptance is recognition of what is. Parents can accept themselves and their children as they are, but they don't have to like or agree with everything that is. People assert themselves when they believe it's right, reasonable, and possible to make changes.

Many books have been written on the topic of assertion which could prove helpful. We have devised the following eight-point guideline for effective assertion from actual counseling experiences, and have found that it works well and is simple to remember.

1. Assert when it is right and reasonable to speak up or do something about a situation. Not to assert can cause frustration, irritability, increased fear, and possibly even depression.
2. Take care not to attack or "put down" the person to whom you are asserting: no name-calling, offensive language, accusations or threats. Use a firm but agreeable tone of voice.
3. Remember asserting is not asking a question or questioning a person's behavior. Neither is it an invitation to a debate or discussion. Asserting is a declarative statement and ends in a period.
4. Begin the assertion with the words, "I would appreciate it if..." It gets you off to the right start.
5. Always assert toward a specific behavior. For example, "I would appreciate it if you would pick up your socks." "I would appreciate it if you would get at the back of the line and wait your turn." " I would appreciate it if you call and let us know if you are not coming into work on time." Phrases such as, "improve your attitude" or "be more considerate" are too vague.
6. A lengthy explanation of why you are asserting is counter-productive. A sentence or two is all that is necessary; otherwise you appear unsure, guilty, or not confident.

7. Call for a "time out" or even excuse yourself for
   a few moments to plan your assertion if you are
   "flustered" or can't immediately think of how to
   assert. Take a deep breath, review these guidelines
   and then come back asserting.
8. Assert once, and if you get no reasonable response,
   assert again in essentially the same way. If no
   response again, then inform the persons that they
   "give you no choice but to" take an alternative action
   if they do not comply. Have in mind your alternative
   action beforehand. Some examples might be to walk
   away, allowing the person to reflect on why they
   could not comply with a reasonable assertion (this
   works well in certain cases, such as with family
   members); discontinue the conversation; refer the
   matter to the manager or supervisor; terminate the
   related agreement or withdraw a privilege; contact
   an attorney or the police. If the person still does not
   comply, then take the alternative action.

Children learn as they grow how to respond to assertions,
and as they do, their relationships expand to encompass wider
boundaries. Parents are individuals who do not have to tolerate
anything their children do at home, either as older adolescents
or young adults. When parents handle their intolerance by
asserting themselves in an adult manner, then valuable lessons
are learned in bringing change about effectively. Of course, if
they are not operating from an independent state of adulthood
themselves (and a lot of parents are not), then the lessons taught
to the children will reflect that lesser state of awareness.

As children are growing up, the number of differences
parents have to tolerate ordinarily diminish. The years of give
and take can leave both parents and adolescents highly skilled
in the process of negotiation, a process which is, again, crucial
to a young adult's ability to get along in school, on the job, in
a relationship, and in society in general. In the process of
growth young people can take on more rights and responsibilities for their own lives, while parents gradually relinquish more
and more authority over children's lives.

If all goes smoothly (and it rarely does), the role of advisor and friend between adults begins to mean more than the role of provider and rule-maker. When children are young, parents have custody, care, and the physical stature to coerce youngsters, usually with the threat of a spanking or some other substitute punishment, or the promise of a desired reward. But as children mature, most parents settle into a routine of modified control within boundaries as the method to obtain cooperation or obedience.

Parents frequently still maintain the authority to hold out some type of punishment or suspension of privileges for the desired motivation. While parents inevitably give up their authority over grown children, some lose the ability to influence intolerable or offensive behavior which goes against their own values or lifestyle, especially in their own home. In fact, this loss is often one of the most important factors in preventing parent-child relationships from moving into adult-adult relationships.

Biologically parents are parents forever; their children will always be their children. Neither parent nor child need renounce that biological relationship in order to expand it and give it new meaning. The young adult can learn to establish his own identity—without denying or renouncing his parents or refusing to recognize and deal with them as adults.

This certainly does not mean parents have to like their children or be liked by them. Parents, too, can learn how to express their own identities as fully functioning, individual adults. When parents are adults, they can share themselves without fear, guilt, jealousy, or displaced anger. What better role model is there for a young person who is well along in the transformation from adolescent to adult? The other option for parents is to share personality deficiencies in their own ignorance and to teach by example the behavior that will ultimately harm their children as it has harmed themselves.

Sometimes anger and frustration over different lifestyles reaches such proportions that it becomes essential to do something about it. There are five ways of handling anger or frustration—two unproductive, two productive, and one in-between. One of the worst ways is to hold it in and do nothing about it. This results in increased anger or frustration and possibly even depression. Just as bad is letting it out destructively by verbally or physically abusing others or destroying property. While destruction may provide some immediate, temporary relief, it leaves a person having to deal with the effects of abuse or destruction such as severed relationships, costs for damages or law suits and with having learned nothing in the process.

The in-between way of handling anger or frustration is to experience a catharsis, or let off steam, by working out the anger or frustration in a physically constructive manner. This can be done, for example, through intense physical exercise such as swimming, beating the couch with a tennis racket, taking a brisk long walk, or getting a massage. Practicing deep relaxation techniques such as diaphragmatic breathing, biofeedback, or meditation following the catharsis is also helpful. Any of these measures can provide necessary relief but not necessarily sufficient release from the basic and often still remaining difficulty.

One of the best ways of dealing with anger and frustration is through effective assertion. Then, not only do people redress the inappropriate and unreasonable behavior in a particular situation, but they also relieve the anger and frustration. Asserting is high level human behavior.

Perhaps the best solution to anger and frustration is not to get angry or frustrated in the first place. People can do this by refuting irrational "shoulds," "oughts," and "musts" and by replacing irrational thinking with more rational self-talk. For example, people can refute "life should be fair" by substituting "life is not always fair." They can refute "he or she should be treating me better" and counter what they are telling themselves with "he or she is treating me poorly and there is nothing I can do (other than assert) to make them treat me better."

Can there really be any doubt that the period when adolescents are becoming adults is also a time for concentrated growth for parents as well? In many ways, parents are being given a second chance to become whole in those areas of life which, for whatever reasons, were not completed earlier. Perhaps parents must undo some habit patterns or change some mental attitudes, because they have told themselves over and over again for years that they are less than adequate or acceptable in some areas. At the heart of many parents' dissatisfaction with who they have become is their misconception of what an adult is.

Whose Home Is It Anyway?

The drama of becoming an adult takes place on many different stage settings, but perhaps the most important set is the home, leading us to focus on the question, "Whose home is it, anyway?" Just as the drama of adolescence is transitory, so is the set of the home where the "coming of age" script is enacted. As we shall see, the set needs to be taken away and a new one put in its place.

Basic understanding of the dynamics involved in becoming adults is important to appreciate why older children living in their parents' home often need to be confronted on the issues of house rules, rights and responsibilities. Parents need to consider whether their home is their children's home without qualification.

What happens if a young person refuses to work, go to school, or takes only one or two college courses at a time? What if they want a boyfriend or girlfriend to move in with them? What if they have parties against their parents' wishes when the parents are not around? What if they frequently leave a spouse or live-in mate or expect to use their parents' home as a stopping place while they change partners?

More often than anyone can imagine, parents come for counseling with such complaints as, "We don't know what to do. Our son has been home for three months and he still isn't working." Increasingly we hear, "She and her two kids have been with us now for four months, but she's still not talking to her husband." Others say, "Even though our son graduated from college four months ago, he's only half-heartedly looking for a job; he says he needs the rest."

We challenge the sacred words, "You ALWAYS have a home with us," and offer an alternative: "Our home is yours to use, as an adult, for a temporary base when necessary." The difference doesn't have to change the quality of caring offered, nor does it limit the joy in having them around or being there for them when genuinely needed.

Parents' homes can be a central place from which children can operate. Parents' homes can be a place for children ordinarily to visit for a few weeks—like two or three, maximum. Parents' homes can be places of refuge, if children are being abused or become disabled or sick, or undergo any emergency. Parents' homes are where children forward their mail when they are in transit. If parents have room, grown children can store some things at their homes, until they are settled in their own places. If they live nearby, children can call before they drop in.

What really underlies understanding the use of the family home is the commitment to the position that being on one's own fosters independence. The more parents encourage older children to be out on their own and communicate confidence in their ability to be on their own, the faster they become separate individuals. Adults are capable of handling their own affairs.

When young adults assume responsibility for their own lives in society, by necessity, they give up the immediate security of their parents' home. Their lives are fundamentally in their own hands, and the last thing they need from parents is mixed messages. So fundamental is the establishment of one's own residence, it is the most obvious symbol of freedom and responsibility for the young adult in society.

If prolonged too much, living at home stifles older adolescents from becoming fully independent adults. Living at home can cause them to regress to immature behavior. When they are living at home, where is the inspiration for independent living?

Following are general guidelines for some of the most common or difficult situations parents and their older children have with respect to living at home. Also, because of recent trends affecting the housing of the elderly, we have included examples of particular interest to grown children and their elderly parents.

Living at Home

Understanding the process of becoming an adult helps parents and young people appreciate the need to separate from each other's influence in order to individuate. Some physical distance can help make the psychological leap to full adulthood easier for many young people and their parents.

Whenever possible, we prefer to see young people move away from home while they attend college or work. Even if the college or their place of employment is in the same town, students or young workers should try to earn enough to contribute towards living away from home. Whether or not they share living expenses with roommates, living away from home is not a waste of money. It's money well spent, whenever it can be arranged, because it promotes independence.

Because housing is so expensive, there is a growing trend for parents to encourage college graduates or the newly employed to live with them, so they can save money. For the reasons we have already stated, we do not recommend this living arrangement unless all other options have failed. We think it is far more valuable for young people to learn to live alone or with one or more peers, sharing expenses and household responsibilities.

If the dishes aren't done, they remain in the sink, until someone other than mother cleans up the kitchen. If the rent isn't paid, the young people face eviction, and should not be bailed out by dad. These are important lessons that are best learned before the responsibility for their own family compounds the difficulties.

The need for a stable, secure, solid, and defined home is psychologically important in the creation of a family environment, especially when raising children. We discourage the attitude that "My parents will take me in, if I can't make it work anymore." The parents may have successfully created a nurturing environment when they raised their children, but it is time for the young person to learn how to do the same thing.

Living with another person is not easy. Relationships shrivel up or fail to grow unless both people renew their efforts at understanding each other and make adjustments frequently. The kind of commitment needed to make a relationship acceptable is not encouraged when one or both people have the attitude that parents are waiting in the wings to bail them out when the going gets tough.

One other caution is exemplified by the case of a student who dropped out of college after doing poorly the first year. More interested in having a good time, he did not apply himself at school. At his mother's insistence, he got a job and was able to meet his personal expenses, buy a new automobile, and in general live a very active social life while living at home.

The young college drop-out did not pay any room or board while he worked and lived at home. At 21, he decided it was time to get serious about higher education and he wanted to return to college. He expected his mother to continue to help by providing free room and board, an offer which had been available four years earlier when he first went to college.

When the young man decided to return to college, the mother was in a dilemma. She was newly remarried to a man who had helped his own four children from a previous marriage through college. Her husband didn't feel it was his or his wife's responsibility to have the young man live with them while he finished college. The son prevailed, and the strain on the new marriage brought the couple in for counseling.

The woman was so filled with guilt concerning her need to help her son that she was unable to see the situation clearly. After some weeks, she came to appreciate that she was not responsible for her son's education anymore. The reasonable offer she had made when he had graduated from high school had been passed by, and she was not bound to keep that offer open on an unlimited basis.

Her life circumstances had, indeed, changed. Although the son's return to college the second time on his own would be more difficult for him financially, it was not impossible. His earning capacity had already been demonstrated in support of his flamboyant life style.

In this case, the mother's guilt and fear of not being a good parent was used unconsciously by the young man to avoid responsibility for himself and his previous decisions. The young man was not intentionally trying to destroy his mother's second marriage, but rather was looking for an easy way to get what he wanted. The problem was the mother's lack of confidence in drawing the line between helping her son, no longer a teenager, or steering him "on his own", so he could help himself.

Vacations and Holidays

We encourage sons and daughters, particularly those in college, to come home for a visit from a few days to a few weeks. That does not mean three or four months of lounging around the house during the summer. Most of us who have ourselves been to college know that the college experience is not abnormally debilitating. It may require intense and periodic effort, and while it certainly can be demanding, for most people college resembles more a summer camp than a concentration camp!

The cry from students for extended recuperation usually accompanies those infamous crash efforts and the midnight study marathons on the part of a disorganized or unfocused student. Crash and cram efforts often make up for the time squandered in areas having little to do with academic achievement, but rather more to do with a last ditch effort to salvage a semester.

Some young people need to learn the hard way what educational psychologists have learned from controlled studies: learning that is distributed or spaced is more efficient in time and retention than learning through massed or crammed practices. Handling the consequences of one's actions, good or bad, is an important part of the experience of managing one's own affairs.

We strongly recommend that young people spend extended holidays and vacations working, either out of the family home or away from it. Being responsible for oneself includes financial and vocational independence. The sooner anyone owns up to that, the better. Working during extended holidays, semester and summer breaks from college provides important mini-experiences at being completely on their own, earning their own room and board, saving to help with tuition and other expenses. Ultimately, this can make the final break with parents less traumatic, because young people will have already experienced minor successes at independence. Also, parents who are less financially capable will welcome the help.

People need to be gainfully employed and be able to make their own way in the world. Supporting themselves is not always easy. Parents who want to shelter their children from the world of work are behaving unrealistically and irrationally. Misguided parenting can lead to unnecessary dependence.

Parents who share the belief that young people should be protected from work as long as possible need to dig a little deeper into their own motivation for perpetuating this dependence. The question they should ask themselves is whether they are protecting the children for their children's' benefit, or for their own need to be parents.

Holidays frequently turn into dreaded occasions when parents insist their children come home for any or all special occasions. That pressure can take the form of tremendous guilt if the children don't oblige. Likewise, children owe their parents the courtesy of asking whether or not their parents want company for the holidays, before they arrive. This applies not only to college aged children, but also to older and middle aged children.

It is surprising how many couples in their thirties and forties come for counseling with complaints that they fight every holiday over whose parents they must visit for the occasion. Young married couples need to establish their own holiday rituals and customs. They can still visit their parents or invite them to visit their home, but it is important that they have some sense of determination where the celebration is concerned. Not to do so is to run the risk that they can't establish their own traditions separate from their parents', or they are unable to assert their own needs over their parents' expectations.

Separation or Divorce

If a couple living together are having difficulty, they should not be encouraged to bring their problems back to the parents. Couples should be encouraged to work out their problems between themselves and seek professional help, if necessary. It is important for parents to avoid involvement in the process of working out these difficulties, since they are rarely impartial. Parents will usually take their children's side in a disagreement and tell them what they want to hear in order to feel better, but not tell them what they need to hear.

A parent's home should not be used as a haven during interpersonal strife in a relationship, except when the difficulties involve what we call the four "A's": addiction to alcohol or drugs, adultery, abandonment, or assault. If any of the four "A's" prevail, professional help is needed.

Parents can assist in obtaining help with the four "A's" by providing a temporary refuge for the abused person, but they are not the best ones to counsel. More often then not, parents in these situations compound the difficulties by feeding into the anger and resentment between the couple. The best assistance parents can give is to insist that the couple get the objective help they need so they can come to their own resolution.

Likewise, if older parents divorce or separate, they should not expect to live with their children. Separation or divorce is not to be taken lightly or encouraged, and the people involved need to assume responsibility for themselves, which might include getting help from social services. Regardless of whether the young people or the parents have made their marital relationships untenable, neither has the right to pressure the other with guilt to take them in when that relationship fails.

But the sword of independence cuts both ways. Children have no more right to pressure their parents with guilt to take them into their homes than parents have to pressure their children to come home. The same principle applies throughout the entire life span. We do not do for our children (or elderly parents or middle aged divorced sons or daughters) what they are capable of doing for themselves. Dependence weakens self-esteem, psychological and physical stamina, and if prolonged unduly, leads to unhealthy or destructive relationships.

The Elderly

In today's society, the same principle of independence applies with respect to elderly parents moving in with their grown children. Because more and more elderly people are capable of handling their own affairs and living independently, they can avoid having to move in with grown children. Most often they are the first to admit that they prefer living independently, when physically possibly. "Adults, no children" is a familiar sign associated with the increasing desire of the elderly to live independently and without hassle.

The increasing number of home health care programs, apartments with supportive services, nursing homes, and older people themselves who have sufficient health, strength, and the means to live on their own have helped stem the obligation to take elderly parents into their children's' homes. Whenever physically possible, we recommend that the elderly live in their own quarters. When nursing home care becomes necessary, it can and should be utilized. It is best to explore alternative/ assistance programs with the elderly before the programs are actually needed.

One case in point occurred when a couple in their late fifties were faced with caring for the husband's disabled mother in the home because the husband insisted they should. The result, which continued for over a year, was a great and unnecessary burden on the wife and their children who were still at home.

Because the family home was modest in size, the living room was converted into a bedroom for the sick woman. The routine of bedpans, constant calls to the doctor, running for medication, preparing special foods, and the increasing dependency on the part of the elderly woman was experienced by everyone in the family. The husband refused to send her to a nursing home, despite the fact that each day she became a greater burden to the son's family and felt guilty as a result.

It took intensive counseling with the couple before the husband was able to perceive his need to drop the parenting role toward his mother and make arrangements for her to be placed in a nursing home. He quickly saw that the care she got there was better than the makeshift arrangements his family was able to provide. The entire family was able to offer more love to the elderly woman during her final days once the obstacles of guilt and resentment were removed.

It is well to remember that part of the dignity of dying and death is to accept the condition of dying and death. Too often the elderly are protected from having to accept their illness and impending death by well-meaning, but misguided family. By refusing to allow the elderly person to face dying and death and by creating distractions and false hopes, the family actually increases the pain. Whenever possible it is helpful to arrange for the elderly to die at home, preferably their own home. "Living Wills" which are drawn up by the elderly while they are still healthy allow them to make decisions about their care when they are dying.

The Sandwich Generation

The dilemma over whether to roll up or roll out the welcome mat in homes is probably most strongly felt by those we call the "sandwich" generation. People in this generation are somewhere in their forties or fifties and are closed in on both sides when it comes to living arrangements. Genevieve and Sam are a case in point.

Married young, Genevieve and Sam had worked hard to provide the best for their two daughters. Their 24 year-old daughter had opted not to go to college and instead became a beautician, subsequently working full time in that capacity. Her 21 year-old sister chose the college route and was about to graduate with a major in elementary education. Unfortunately, she failed the teacher certification test and would have to wait several months before testing again. In the meantime, she was without work.

Both young women had always lived at home. Genevieve and Sam graciously accepted the living arrangements, but in their quiet hours admitted to each other that they were looking forward to the time when their daughters would be married or well employed and out of the house. The feeling of being "home free" and having the opportunity to renew their romance with each other had begun to rise. Not too high, though.

Sam's father began to have problems. Up until this time, the father had managed quite well for himself, but his eyesight was fading and severe arthritis made it difficult to do many household chores. Sam had grown up with his own grandfather living in his father's household. He felt the custom of taking elderly parents into the home was not only an honorable custom, but the right thing to do.

Sam saw no alternative but to invite his own father to live with him now that the older man was having physical problems. Sam's brothers and sisters, who lived out of town, also thought it best that Sam do his duty. Genevieve did not like the idea one bit.

Meanwhile the daughters had convinced Genevieve and Sam that the world was a hard cruel place when it came to renting or buying a house. The parents agreed that the cost of housing had skyrocketed during the last decade. It seemed to make sense that the daughters should continue to live at home.

The silent dissatisfaction and frustration that Genevieve and Sam experienced began to spread. They started arguing with each other continually. Sam parried Genevieve's suggestion that his father find another living arrangement by pointing out that they were only doing for his father what they were doing for their daughters.

The second honeymoon was off, and they came for counseling frustrated, depressed, and contemplating divorce. The "sandwich" they found themselves in was held together by their "shoulds," "oughts," and "musts" regarding their obligations to provide housing for others. An interesting breakthrough occurred for them when they both admitted that they would not want or expect their daughters to take them into their homes when they were old, nor did either of them ever live at home with their own parents after they had graduated from school.

Over the years they had rationalized the dissonance they felt regarding independence, had given in to the pressure from those around them to support family no matter what, and had convinced themselves that they "should" roll out the welcome mat to daughters and dad alike. Refuting the "shoulds" involved that they first see how their actions were protracting the dependence of their daughters and initiating dependence in Sam's father.

In both cases, Sam and Genevieve were undermining the confidence and self-respect of the daughters and the father. In the process, they had failed to realize that the values of the extended family belonged to another era. Because of such support systems as social security, a more equitable workforce and a prosperous economy, and numerous alternative living arrangements for the young and the old alike, Sam and Genevieve did not have to provide housing for the next or the last generation.

Eventually, they worked through their dilemma. The daughters, after failing in a last ditch guilt trip, agreed it probably was best for them to move out and face the world. Sam's father moved into an apartment complex that provided maintenance free living, meals, a social program, and immediate medical attention if necessary. The family continued to see each other regularly and Sam and Genevieve actually did go on a second honeymoon.

More Examples of Irksome Home Behavior

So often in dealing with maturing adolescents or elderly parents, we find less difficulty with the serious problems than we do in handling day-to-day irritations. But we have found that when we avoid handling the day-to-day annoyances, we allow a crisis to smolder. Then suddenly, a seemingly minor infraction causes someone to erupt in anger, but that anger really reflects a collection of frustrations that had not been addressed previously.

Six simple steps can help alleviate misunderstandings:

1. Honestly ask yourself, "What is really bothering me?"
2. Understand where the annoyance came from, how it is affecting you now, and what will happen if you continue to hold onto it.
3. Accept responsibility for your part in the misunderstanding and don't merely blame other people, situations, or things for the difficulty.
4. Identify and refute the irrational "shoulds," "oughts," and "musts" that you are telling yourself because they are causing you to feel the way you do.
5. Assert yourself. Take whatever action seems right and reasonable to resolve the problem.
6. Accept what you cannot change.

One couple, who had lived in a warm climate, found it extremely difficult when the woman's retired parents arrived for their annual six-week visit in order to avoid the worst of the winter months up north. The woman's father had brusque manners, and he constantly picked on his dependent wife.

Although the couple had always been able to overlook the older man's annoying habits and accept him as he was, they could not tolerate it when he began to criticize the son-in-law in the same way he picked on his own wife. Instead of confronting the older man immediately and resolving the issue before it got worse, the husband tried to ignore the attacks. Finally the older man became so abusive that the husband asserted himself and gave him the ultimatum to stop or leave, whereupon the older man left in anger with his passive wife in tow.

The couple learned that even though the father-in-law's behavior had been tolerated by others all his life, they need not tolerate it in their own home. In fact, to do so was to cater to the older man's immature behavior. It is unfortunate that no one had stood up to the older man earlier in his life, which might have helped him to overcome his bullying behavior. It was also important that the couple understand that their refusal to tolerate the behavior was within their rights as hosts.

Here are some other situations which pose opportunities for assertion and change. Not all of them are a concern in every home. They merely represent some of the issues which come up frequently. In any case, remember, your home is not your grown children's or your parent's home where they can do anything they want. Such as, perhaps:

> Leave lights burning indiscriminately and wastefully around the house. Take long hot showers, especially in the morning when the last person goes without hot water. Overuse the telephone, tying the lines up for hours. Run up long distance telephone charges with no intention of paying for them.

Take whatever one wants from the refrigerator, without regard to whether it's for a planned meal. Eat or behave at table like small or squabbling children. Smoke or drink around the house when it has been requested not to do so. Refuse to clean up after oneself or mess up rooms shared by everyone in the house.

Play music loudly, especially at inappropriate times. Monopolize television programs without considering others' preferences. Have parties in the home, which the home owners don't approve of. Don't show up (or show up!) for meals without notification.

Use someone else's automobile without permission or concern for anyone else's inconvenience. Drive carelessly or dangerously or without showing regard for the maintenance of the car. Refuse to use public transportation, but insist on being chauffeured.

Use charge cards without permission. Borrow things around the house and never return them. Flaunt opposing attitudes or use offensive language, without consideration for whose home it is. Leave condoms or other contraceptives, drug paraphernalia, or alcohol bottles plainly in view around the house when requested not to.

Parents do not have to permit it or look the other way when their daughter or son wants to take a boyfriend or girlfriend up to the bedroom for several hours with the door shut. Whether they go elsewhere and engage in sex is beyond the parent's influence. But parents do not have to stand by silently, knowing full well that their home has made possible behavior they disapprove of.

If parents' values do not include premarital sex, they should stand firm on what they believe. If premarital or extramarital sex is acceptable to parents, then they should not object when others engage in those behaviors. The same applies to homosexuality, abortions, divorce, or any other value judgements people hold regarding interpersonal behavior.

Finally, we want to call attention to an alarming trend based upon the latest information from the Census Bureau. In 1970, 9.5 percent of all men aged 25-34 lived with their parents. By 1990 that was up to 15 percent. Among women, the two-decade rise was far more gradual, from 6.6 percent in 1970 to 8.1 percent in 1990. Within this same age group in 1990, 32 percent of single men (that's 1 out of 3) and 20 percent of single women (that's 1 out of 5) were living with their parents.

Whether the reason people accept this trend is tough economic times or later marriages, convenience, comfort or fear, it is a phenomenon that hampers adult independence for sons and daughters as well as parents. This is precisely the sort of trend that reinforces our concern that Americans are protracting adolescence too long.

The week after The New York Times reported the census comparisons, a gentleman responded with a letter to the editor encouraging parents to push fledglings out of the nest—for everybody's sake. Not to do so cripples and arrests development and deprives them of the necessity to come to terms with limits and self-responsibility. Not to do so also deprives parents from working out their own companionship and personal needs that may have been tabled during the time children were growing up.

Three cheers for him! We could not have summarized it better. Perhaps there is indeed light at the end of the dependency tunnel. And maybe we can roll up the welcome mats and move on with independent adult living after all.

Chapter Four
Entitlements and Education:
A Hard Line on the Bottom Line

The application of bottom line thinking to the development process illustrates the necessity for vocational/ financial independence as an important step in gaining satisfaction, confidence, security, and self-esteem. Chapter Four gets down to the nitty gritty details of who pays for what and the hidden expectations often attached to the bottom line. Critical issues in education set the stage for how excessive or unnecessary financial support, especially without emotional and personal independence, produces a sense of fear-based entitlement which inevitably leads to conflict. College myths such as "college for everybody" and "college is a good place to learn independence" are questioned. Expectations of people in financial difficulties who assume others owe them a start in life, regular help in acquiring material goods, or assistance in surviving marital/familial problems are examined. Discussion also focuses on the elderly who are made unnecessarily dependent by over-extended helping hands that deny them the opportunity to be on their own and maintain their self-respect.

If we do not establish ourselves as separate, independent, individuated adults, vocationally and financially, we will be stuck defending ourselves from incompetence, failure, and fear of abandonment and the subsequent depression associated with having to be on our own. In effect, we won't grow up.

When people are vocationally independent, they have chosen a means of employment that they like and enjoy. They either have the skills to perform their chosen activity or they can learn the required skills. Also their vocational choice is practical in terms of money, demand, and geographical location. When someone does something he doesn't like or something which isn't economically in demand, or which he isn't qualified to do, he is vocationally dependent.

Able and competent adults are not regularly dependent on others for their financial resources, although they can accept help that is freely offered and does not undermine their development and independence. They do not trade their independence or integrity for someone's promises to take care of them financially. Financial, vocational and educational "entitlements" can stand in the way of being on their own.

Finding Your Niche

One phrase that keeps appearing throughout much development literature is "second chance." Whether it refers to the time when young people are passing into adulthood or later in life when older individuals are fully embracing tasks which were left undone during their own transition to adulthood, it is still a second chance to become a whole person.

In 1970 when Erik Erikson forecast a "revolt of the dependent," society was ill-prepared for how thoroughly those words would apply decades later. Today, the economically dependent (the poor) and the culturally dependent (minority groups) are demanding more rights and opportunities to realize their potential. Also, one trip to a bookstore will reveal a whole new section dedicated to those who suffer from what we now call co-dependency.

When Erikson first referred to the developmentally dependent, he meant young people looking for more of their share of power and goods. But it is easy to extend the group to include all those who suffer from inadequate psychological development or immaturity. In other words, those who have not yet become fully adult.

Chronological age offers no guarantee that someone has successfully made the rite of passage from adolescence to adulthood. What makes today's environment so exciting is that people from 18 to 100 years are admitting their developmental deficiencies and taking the necessary steps to remove those obstacles that have stifled and blocked their growth.

Parents have a tendency to become over-involved in their children's lives at three critical stages in life: when the children are approaching the end of adolescence and are resisting the transition to adulthood, when the children are middle aged and facing a crisis at home or at work, and when the parents are elderly and facing a crisis in their own lives and look to their children for help. The failure to separate from parents sometimes reflects overindulgence on the part of the parents, which almost always makes it more difficult for the older child to become independent, and usually symbolizes the parents' own fear of abandonment by their son or daughter.

We have already said that the most difficult area of development involves ego/emotional independence. But frequently, the step before achieving ego/emotional independence involves overcoming vocational dependence. Hence, we want to take a hard look at the bottom line of vocational independence and some of the factors that are making it extremely difficult for individuals to separate financially and vocationally.

Remember we said that the key issue to be resolved when moving from adolescence to adulthood is identity. People should not have to sacrifice or compromise individual identity in order to earn a living. It is far more effective to find the kind of work they like, work which capitalizes on their talents and skills, rather than work that requires them to change their nature.

In psychology there is a term called foreclosure that describes an ineffective way someone deals with pressure from other significant people. Foreclosure often involves vocational choices. Rather than confront the stress and conflict of making career commitments out of personal conviction, a person caves in and uncritically complies with what stronger personalities want him or her to do.

Identity foreclosure often characterizes the lives of obedient, approval-oriented people. They trade security, praise, and acceptance for their own personal commitment. They go to the schools and major in the courses of study chosen for them by someone else. Or they take the job in the family business, or with a firm that was arranged for them because they are too afraid to challenge authority or the roles chosen for them. They can even go through their entire lives and never find out what they themselves want to do for themselves. Recent estimates are that two out of three people do not like their jobs.

When it comes to vocational decisions, time and again we have offered the following three guidelines in order of importance. All three need to be present for complete independence to occur.

1. Do something you enjoy.
2. Do something for which you have the skills or for which you can acquire the skills.
3. Do something practical and geographically feasible which will allow you to support yourself, either because it is in demand or a demand can be stimulated.

Along the way people may have to temporarily take jobs that do not fit the above criteria, but these temporary stops are stepping stones to a goal they have formulated for themselves. And, yes, that goal may change many times throughout a lifetime. But when they start changing their values, study subjects they are not really interested in, give up satisfying activities, or significantly alter their behavior just to get a job, they are headed for a painful identity crisis. When they avoid independence in the vocational area, they have set the stage for avoiding separation-individuation and never becoming adults.

Who Pays for What

Any discussion of the bottom line must deal with the hidden expectations that are attached to it. Parents who help their older sons and daughters acquire material goods, invite them to live at home as long as they like, or foot entire bills for higher education, often expect to be paid back—but not in cash. Frequently the pay-back comes when parents demand respect or expect ideal behavior from their children. This kind of thinking leads parents to interfere later in the domestic relations of their children or to harbor the expectation that they will be taken care of by their children in their old age.

In a relationship between life partners, often the financial provider **expects** forgiveness, obedience, gratitude, and no resistance to unacceptable behavior. The financially dependent person lacks confidence and is insecure because he or she is so trapped in the fear of separation or abandonment. Such unwarranted expectations lead to dishonest behavior with one person looking the other way to keep things secure and the other demanding things "should be" his or her way. The self-inflated financial importance of the one person is as much an ego defense as the whining, blaming, and complaining of the dependent partner.

Likewise in society, excessive financial support, instead of promoting emotional and personal independence, produces what we call fear-based entitlement. When financial fears dominate people's lives, entitlements, such as welfare, are demanded and expected. The threat of having entitlements taken away is met with anger, withdrawal of political support, and even violence.

This is not to say one can't give financial assistance to those who need help getting started or in times of temporary crisis. But did anyone **really** believe we could promote independence in the major areas of life by handing out welfare payments to two and three generations of the same families or blank checks to adolescents without providing opportunities to develop the skills that promote adult responsibility? Sooner or later, suppressed feelings of anger, guilt, or jealousy based upon a lack of personal achievement and confidence rise to the surface. Finding no satisfaction on the surface, there is no place to go but the depths—depression.

Finances and the 18-25 year-olds

In discussing financial support for this age group, we'll break the group into two categories, those who go to college and those who don't. But whether someone goes to college or not, the same principles for independence apply.

According to the American Council on Education, at the end of the last decade about 11.6 million families in the United States—18 percent of all families—had one or more members between the ages of 18 and 24. Of these families, about 35 percent had one or more such members attending college full-time. The Department of Education estimated that about 12.5 million students of all ages were enrolled in higher education at that time.

The National Center for Education Statistics set a $24 billion figure as the amount spent in 1987 for college tuition and fee payments. The Consumer Expenditure Survey by the Bureau of Labor Statistics indicated that $18 billion of direct payments for college tuition and fees that year came from households. Is there any doubt that Americans are willing to sacrifice financially to provide for what they believe is a distinct advantage—a college education? The U.S. Census figures indicated that 20 percent of those 25 years or older had baccalaureate degrees, a percentage that climbs slowly every year, with almost a million more graduates annually.

Almost half of the nation's tuition bills are paid by householders aged 45-64, presumably for their children. Almost 20 percent are paid by householders under the age of 25, most likely a college student paying for his or her own education. It seems safe to assume that the middle aged and the middle class are paying the bulk in tuition costs in America.

And the squeeze is on the middle class. The wealthy can pay the full amount and it doesn't hurt. The poor who qualify can get need-based financial assistance so it doesn't hurt either. But the middle class pays until it hurts. Colleges and lending institutions now make their financial allocations based upon parents' ability to borrow—and borrow heavily.

The trend for more education was fed by the rising incomes of parents and their commitment to spend more on improving their children's lives rather than having more children. The trend was also fed by more public supported schooling opportunities and subsidies such as scholarships, loans, the G.I. bill, and the perceived value of education, both socially and in potential income.

But the mystique surrounding higher education has also effectively resulted in more parents subsidizing longer periods of dependency in order to get their children through college. This lengthened transition to adulthood has created special problems of identity and role responsibility. We think it's time to reevaluate who pays for what, in an effort to clarify some of the role confusion.

If parents willingly accept responsibility for the cost of tuition, room, board, transportation, and miscellaneous expenses, including entertainment for their son or daughter at college, they are encouraging dependence. They certainly have a vested interest in the student's success, and may even get vicarious satisfaction from the student's performance and the reputation of the schools attended by their children. But they also have a concerned financial interest in the choice of the college or university.

Just because a student gets a "good feeling" at a high priced, private, small, exclusive, prestigious institution doesn't mean parents have to pay twice as much to send their son or daughter there. Parents have rights as well as responsibilities, something they may need to remind themselves of from time to time. One of the marks of adulthood is the ability to accept challenge and denial. If Johnny's parents won't foot the bill for Johnny to go to High Cost U., but they will send him to State University, let Johnny figure out how to make up the difference if it's High Cost U. he demands.

Likewise, if Johnny knows he would hate going to the expensive, prestigious school, but he might do well at a less high-powered institution, he may need help resisting his parents. Being unable to resist the pressure from parents isn't going to help Johnny become an adult, regardless of whether he buckles down and eventually graduates from the college his parents have chosen for him.

Everyone has become sharply aware of the astronomical cost of a college education. We received a brochure from an institution saying, "You can afford to send your daughter or son to Big Name University." The total cost for one year tuition, room, and board was over $23,000, a four-year outlay of $92,000 or more, or the equivalent cost of a home in many American locales or a new luxury car every year that has no trade-in value.

After reading the fine print, we discovered that the tuition assistance plan at Big Name University was indeed a loan financed with something like a second mortgage on the parents' home. Rather ominous prospects for those who have more than one college-bound child. Raising children used to be thought of as primarily a time commitment. Now it seems to be primarily a money commitment, and plenty of it at that.

Of course banks and universities want parents to accept full responsibility for higher education. Education is one of the biggest businesses in America today. But one should not lose sight of the fact that many of these special interest groups regard education as a product to be sold to the public. Enrollment pays the bills and keeps the institutions solvent, no matter how lofty the speeches, or what kind of pressure they apply, or even whether the finished product— the student—actually learned anything of value or is capable of earning a living, or is satisfied with the education received.

Yet the cost of college doesn't have to be astronomical for parents. Public universities are state subsidized by taxes (which parents pay) in order to reduce the actual cost of tuition paid directly by students to attend the institution. As a result, publicly supported schools can cost half that of independent schools.

While it is true that many of the nation's top colleges and universities are endowed, private institutions, it is also true that numerous "flagship" state colleges and universities offer comparable education. Often state-subsidized schools have more money for faculty and facilities than the average independent institution, which must use tuition and donations to cover all operating expenses.

Do some research with the aid of books, libraries, higher education periodicals, and high school and college placement counselors. Parents owe it to themselves to make informed choices and save money, too. Keep in mind that more than half a million students now transfer annually to four-year institutions, half of them from economical community colleges, which account for half of all entering first-year students into higher education.

Young people also have the privilege of choice, but they need to remember that privileges come with responsibilities. Students, who insist on prestigious and expensive institutions, can pay the additional fees through loans or money they earn working part-time during school and full-time during vacations if they want to attend those colleges or universities badly enough. If they so choose, they will probably value their education more and work harder for it.

A careful review of such statistics as grade point averages, scholastic aptitude scores of entering college freshmen, scores on national achievement tests, faculty qualifications, student satisfaction ratings, subsequent job placement and salaries generally reveals no significant differences between the average publicly supported college and the average private college or university. No significant difference except one—cost—since private colleges can cost twice as much.

That's all the more reason why middle class parents and students need to choose carefully. Parents should not get swept up in emotions such as wanting only the very best for "our Johnny." All parents want the best for their children. If Johnny is an average to very good student, he will do just fine at State University or a small moderately priced institution. Branch campuses and community colleges are good alternatives for those who want to gradually work up to full size universities, either public or private.

Parents who are middle class and have a very bright student can work all the angles to ensure maximum merit-based assistance. We know one family who worked with four comparable top-flight schools, openly sending copies of each school's offer to their competitors. In this way they gradually increased the amount of aid offered until they chose the school that provided the best all-round assistance package.

Students can reasonably earn enough money to pay for most, if not all, of their own room and board, books, supplies, entertainment, clothes and transportation expenses. They can earn $3000-$5000 working part-time during school and full-time during the summer, holidays, and mid-semester "breaks."

There are numerous part-time minimum wage service jobs available. There are also more lucrative jobs, usually involving tips (waiter, waitress, bellhop, coat-check), which should be considered. More and more businesses are devising ways to give students work experiences related to their major course of study during the summer holidays. It is interesting that in many ways, businesses are taking the lead in educational reforms in the 90s.

Our philosophy with regard to students' working is that no legitimate job should be considered beneath them. Our experience verifies that students often learn more interpersonal skills from summer waiter-waitress work than they do from classroom lectures on working with people. Ironically, many of the college professors teaching the courses have never had any experience working in the "real" world to begin with.

Students who have worked and borrowed money to attend college also have more incentive to find a job to pay back loans after they graduate, rather than "hang out" or rest up after their senior year and see what happens. They know from experience what it is like to earn money and balance a budget. When the bills come in, they know what it is to be responsible, and they understand what happens when cash runs out. They can't just call home for more. Money and time management are part of a well-rounded education.

When students clearly understand and accept financial responsibility for their own education, parents can assume responsibility for such things as tuition, health insurance, and perhaps automobile insurance or major car repairs, if they wish. One family we know set a $5000 limit (a limit—not an allowance) for assistance for each of their three students attending college. The students were taught how to list all sources of income, including grants, loans, scholarships, personal savings, money from parents, and any income expected from part-time jobs.

Then all their expenses were listed, including tuition, fees, room and board, books, transportation, insurance and medical expenses, laundry and toiletries, car upkeep, gas, entertainment, clothes, trips home, weekend trips, and any other personal expenses expected. After allocating income against projected expenses the students had their first taste of realistically appraising their own ability to maintain their lifestyle. Did they get everything they wanted? No. Did they get what they needed and valued most? Yes. Did the parents and the students each understand their commitments to each other? Clearly and specifically.

In the case of this family, the son earned a merit scholarship which subsidized more expensive tuition at the college of his choice. One daughter earned a partial basketball scholarship at the small independent college of her choice. The other daughter, who didn't earn any scholarships, attended a state university. Each knew the budgetary limits and worked at part-time jobs to meet needs. They all graduated with a small amount of debt and a great deal of satisfaction knowing they had played a significant part in obtaining their own education.

We encourage students to take out education loans and pay them back themselves after they graduate. The loans offset above average costs and other expenses and are government supported and available to anyone. Students sign for and are responsible for the loans, not parents. We discourage parents from co-signing for other loans, which reinforces financial dependency, and increases the possibility for conflict if the loans are not paid back on time. Students might find it too easy to put off paying their parents when it's time to repay loans, especially if they don't particularly value their education to begin with.

Another quite different example involved a single mother and her 21 year-old son who was to graduate from a local college in May. She had planned an expensive graduation celebration in his honor. The mother had paid for the young man's entire education, provided him an allowance, and never expected him to contribute financially or even physically towards life at home. She felt he was a fine young man and a good son who gave her no disciplinary problems and maintained average performance at school.

Two weeks before the celebration, the son said the college wasn't going to allow him to graduate on time. The mother simply could not understand how the college could have allowed her son to get into the position of not graduating on time when he did not have enough credits the last semester. When she called the registrar at the college herself, she was surprised to learn that her son had known all along that he would not be able to graduate.

What this mother and son came to understand was that he was afraid to graduate. He knew he was expected to get a job, move out, and be on his own. He had so little experience with responsibility, other than scholastic, that he secretly sabotaged his own graduation by not taking enough credits. In a systematic way, a plan was developed to help this young man quickly gain the missing credits and get a job that would enable him to separate from his mother and be on his own.

College is NOT for Everyone (Nor is it Always the Best Place to Learn Independence)

A case in point involved an athletic young man named Joe who was a sophomore student in one of our classes in college. Unfortunately he was failing the course, so he was invited in to talk about his situation. He revealed that he hated going to college. Joe was the first son from a large family and the pride of his father, a steel worker, who had saved all his life to give his son the advantages of a college education. Joe was filled with frustration and an overwhelming sense of guilt because he didn't want to fulfill his father's dream for him.

It had never crossed Joe's mind not to work while he was going to school. During the past two summers, he was a carpenter's apprentice, and he loved every minute on the job. Each morning he woke up looking forward to his work and ended each day filled with pride and satisfaction—just the opposite of how he felt during the academic year. Already he was making good money and realized the prospect for much more, a prospect which he sincerely doubted his degree in business administration would equal. Also, he dreaded being cooped up in an office for the rest of his life.

For Joe, the best advice we could give was to take the same construction job during the upcoming summer. If he still felt the same way about his job and school at the end of the summer, he should seriously consider not returning to college, but instead continue his apprenticeship. We never saw Joe again on campus, but we did receive a letter two years later from a grateful and responsible young adult who had begun his own construction business and was about to get married. Eventually Joe's father accepted his decision and admitted that college was not synonymous with success.

Back in the early 1970s, educators made some prophetic statements and recommendations based upon such information as the "Report of the Panel on Youth of the President's Science Advisory Committee." This particular report recognized fundamental deficiencies in educational practices which isolate young people in schools that are out of touch with the world of work and society in general. Subsequently, many others who specialize in the transformation of children into adults have suggested that society was headed for trouble unless some major changes were made in the way youth are educated even before they reach the age of 18. Twenty years later some of those alarming trends that were predicted are evident.

Young people need alternative environments, including responsible work and social experiences, to develop the skills which learned knowledge provides. Exposure to a variety of interpersonal experiences also contributes to emotional maturity. We are convinced that without this full range of experiences and responsibilities, young people fail to become adults.

An esteemed psychologist, Erik Erikson, identified eight critical periods during a person's life. One example is when an infant develops basic trust over basic mistrust. Erikson showed how the outcome of each critical encounter determines whether a person will experience growth or regression in life. A critical development issue for adolescents, echoed by many in the field of psychology, is whether they form their own identity or flounder in role confusion, often for a lifetime.

When a person successfully resolves the identity crisis, then an intimate relationship with another person is possible without risking the loss of one's own identity. The passage to adulthood is well on its way. But if the task is not achieved during the proper time, between approximately 18-24 years of age, it will not be achieved well, and could even cause partial or complete failure in other critical tasks to come.

Many educators and social scientists have been calling attention to forces in society that have created an adolescent culture that is spinning out of control. In efforts to protect young people while they prepare for the transition to adulthood, everyone—including parents, educators, and politicians—has gone too far. The very ideas and institutions created to serve the genuine needs of young people have isolated them and deprived them of experiences they need to grow and develop.

For example, labor and wage laws designed to protect youth from harm have become so cumbersome that it is difficult for them to even get work experience. Employers are discouraged from hiring young people because federal and state regulations limit job flexibility, set relatively high minimum wages, or require special insurances and difficult administrative procedures.

Too many parents have given young people material advantages as a substitute for real human contact, something the parents may never have experienced themselves. There is little incentive for adolescents to satisfy their own material needs, and instead, they feel inadequate and incapable of fitting into a world they view with increasing fear, hostility, and cynicism.

Also, because schools are compartmentalized and rigidly structured, there is little opportunity for parent substitutes to assume the role of mentors to young people, modelling mature behavior, and passing on vital skills, culture, ideas, and information between different age groups. Young people need more opportunities to manage their own affairs within a structured environment at home, at school, and on the job. Educators need to incorporate ways to involve young people in organizations and public services that benefit others and enable them to develop leadership skills and responsibility.

Educators, who are rarely rewarded for success in providing knowledge, are even more rarely punished for poor teaching. They have little outside motivation to find new or better ways to teach or to change a system that protects their privileged and isolated ivory towers of learning. Many people today question the soaring cost of education that has produced a large group of highly schooled but under-educated, underemployed, and disappointed people.

One educational observer, Frank Cardelle, summed up the problem succinctly. Our schools are factories; our teachers merely trainer-technicians; our youth force a commodity that is bartered with grades, scholarships, and future financial rewards. The hard-driven competitive student is the loser in a society that puts things before people, profit before health, and image before reality.

The litany of frightening trends of self-destruction, ranging from the abuse of drugs and alcohol to alarming increases in suicide, scream for reforms in education because that is where the bulk of childhood and adolescence is spent. Without adequate exposure to the realities of the world, complete with competent adult role models, how can adolescents become independent physically, intellectually, socially, morally, and in the financial/vocational, and ego/emotional areas?

Our prescription for independence between the ages of 18 to 25 years echoes many of the recommendations based upon reports such as that of the President's Science Advisory Committee. Of course, society needs to have required goods and services produced, but we also need to have socially valued work performed–not just for the benefit of society, but because individuals grow from experiences of responsibility that affect other people. If people are not to be crippled during the transformation from adolescence to adulthood, educators need to move faster on the kinds of changes that were identified decades ago—changes that promote adulthood.

No matter how many unresolved developmental issues must be worked through for complete separation-individuation to occur in the major areas of life, it is never too late. The bottom-line rewards of adulthood are independence, self-esteem, and freedom to be oneself, not merely grades, awards, and money.

Admittedly, American colleges try to be all things to everybody and in the process often produce graduates who are no more prepared to support themselves than they were when they started. The notion that college is the ticket or key to jobs and successful living has led many disillusioned and frustrated people down the arduous obstacle course of useless college course requirements. Except for technical or specialized areas, most employers aren't as concerned with a student's major, as they are with the fact that someone has a degree and can learn.

So why is the degree so important? Perhaps because Americans have protracted adolescence so long that the degree is, at least, one way for an employer to know that the person was able to get through the academic obstacle course. A graduate, presumably, is then capable of being trained by the company to do the required job. Also since there is no guarantee anymore that a high school graduate is even literate, at least it is fairly safe to assume that a college graduate is. What a sad commentary on education.

Our point is not that we get rid of higher education, but rather that the vocational mystique surrounding higher education is a fantasy. The reality doesn't hold up to the ideal as so many frustrated graduates are finding out when they enter (or can't enter) the marketplace. Alarming statistics on unemployed college graduates and people who are dissatisfied vocationally leads us to question the value of college for everybody.

What is important is that people examine their motives for sending children to college or for attending college themselves. Are they forcing themselves or others through the education factories with the promise of economic success as the carrot that motivates—a promise which is being viewed with increasing suspicion? Have people brainwashed themselves and forced themselves and others into colleges they hate attending, where they learn as little as they can get away with, and at best, graduate—still rebellious adolescents? Are people afraid, for themselves or their children, to reject the college myths in order to try some alternative educational experiences?

College faculty and administrators have openly voiced their concern, or quietly discussed among themselves, that many colleges have become "holding tanks" or "baby-sitters" for too many young people who are waiting to grow up. Families expect colleges to "care for" an increasing number of students who show little or no enthusiasm for the academic programs or even the traditional extra-curricular activities such as sports, clubs, student government, media, and theater. The faculty are responsible for stimulating and motivating indifferent students and they cannot assume that students are in college to learn. The administration tries to provide increasingly more lavish entertainment, state of the art accommodations, and gourmet cafeteria food in order to attract students and remain competitive.

Both faculty and administration recognize and lament the increased boredom, immaturity, and dependency of many students. A whole array of social, economic, psychological, and even legal services are offered to "bail out" troubled students. The womb of college life once again reinforces the nineties version of the "in loco parentis" role of colleges and dependency problems continue. Students who are bored and resentful of the "baby-sitter" mentality of colleges can take courage and get out. They can find a college or university that promotes independence or go "on their own" and return to college later when they are ready and if they desire.

Being "on their own" in the world of work would be a far better education for many students at this stage in life—an education in self-reliance, maturity, and an appreciation for the economic reality of money and what it buys. Faculty who have taught older mature students who have returned to college or adult continuing education can vouch for the motivation and appreciation adults have for learning.

Despite all these concerns, college hasn't lost its attraction. Parents who have not gone to college often believe it promises a better life for their children. Those who have gone to college wonder if that is really so, but they are not likely to buck the system either. Even if they snicker at the ivory tower rationale that academic freedom must be protected from the competitive influences of the "real world", or they envy the college faculty's three month vacations in the summer, the month-long paid semester breaks, the paid sabbatical every seven years, the generous salaries for the 15-20 hour required work week, the system of tenure that prevents dismissal, the laid-back, country club campus atmosphere; even so, parents put cash on the line and buy into the system.

College isn't for everybody, and it often isn't a good place to learn independence. Learning can take place at any time and anywhere in life. Some colleges and universities are recognizing the value of life experiences and devising ways to integrate those experiences into accredited programs. People who were not ready for formal education when they passed through adolescence are quite ready at a later time in life. Knowledgeable administrators in education are making it easier for people to move in and out of formal education throughout the entire life span.

For those who go to work straight out of high school, we strongly recommend that they pay room and board to their parents if they live at home. We have already recommended elsewhere that they not live at home if they can make other arrangements. We had one case where a young woman worked, lived at home without any financial obligation to her parents, and established a habit of uncontrolled spending. She never saved any of her paycheck, and if she overspent and couldn't pay her charge accounts, her mother bailed her out.

In this case, the daughter finally left home at 27, resenting her parents' interference in her life. The habit of uncontrolled spending was so ingrained, however, that she had to seek assistance from one of her sisters who saw the problem more clearly. The sister obtained power of attorney in the young woman's behalf, stopped all lines of credit, enforced a strict budget, and began the step by step process of teaching her sister through experience the skills of personal money management, including paying her rent on time.

Whether people choose to go to college or not, go to a vocational-technical school, or get a job directly, they learn more and grow more from the way they adapt to financial/ vocational challenges which often include setbacks, losses, or disappointments, rather than unnecessary support and bail-outs. Character development on the way to becoming an adult enables them to handle challenge and denial. That type of character building does not happen unless they are exposed to real-world experiences and that includes working and earning a living.

For the 25 to 65 year-olds

Individuals in the 25 to 65 year-old range need to abide by the same principles that foster adulthood for 18 to 25 year-olds. Help them without doing anything for them that they can do themselves. Also, as much as possible, allow them to experience the consequences of their own behavior.

We caution relatives of someone in this age group not to provide money, food, clothing, and shelter on a regular basis, and that includes the down payment on their first home, that they can provide themselves. Don't bail them out of financial jams that they have irresponsibly gotten themselves into, such as defaulted loans or credit card abuses. Take a hard line on the bottom line here, even if it means they go without many of the conveniences and luxuries that society has come to regard as essentials.

The real essentials are food, clothing, and shelter, but not dining out, designer fashions, or suburban split level homes in the right section of town. If non-essentials have to go, then they have to go for the greater and more important lesson to be learned. That lesson could be learned as a result of the repossession of a home or car, or the loss of credit and bankruptcy.

Obviously, few people can stand by completely hardened to the financial difficulties of family. There will be exceptions— times when one-time assistance is necessary in an emergency situation or extraordinary generosity in recognition of life's significant events is due, but that is quite different from reinforcing a pattern of irresponsibility. Regrettably, those who consistently bail others out contribute to the problems of irresponsibility.

Fortunately Americans live in an economy where there is food, clothing, and shelter available for those willing to face their fears and work for it. The social service system is available for emergency relief, but it was never intended to be the way of life it has become for many. Resources would be better spent teaching skills, following up with job placement, even creating meaningful jobs, and helping those less fortunate to help themselves, rather than providing money to the point where entitlement becomes the norm. We also question the notion that provides sustained financial benefits to the unemployed who refuse jobs outside their geographic area or their area of expertise.

Parents, or the grown children of parents who expect financial support, don't want to turn a deaf ear to family members in financial trouble, nor should they. The financial trouble, however, may be just the tip of a psychological iceberg. If people have the means themselves, they can always offer to help family members to help themselves.

For example, they can subsidize or assist in providing for education or skills training. They can help family members in need to find programs for self-improvement and even help pay for rehabilitation counseling when it is required. We emphasize that the individuals in need should do as much as possible for themselves, including taking loans, adjusting lifestyles, and being responsible for their own lives. People receiving this type of help need to experience the consequences of their behavior throughout the entire process.

The following case illustrates how hidden expectations attached to the bottom line can reinforce and cause dependency and conflict in a relationship. Grace was an attractive, intelligent, forty year-old woman who held a steady job at a utility company for more than ten years. Over the years she had been promoted in the company to a supervisory position which paid a good salary. Her live-in boyfriend, Peter, a self-styled inventor, called himself the creative one in the relationship. He never paid his share financially for rent, food, or utilities and rarely held any job for more than one year. He was waiting for one of his inventions to bring in the "big bucks."

If Peter needed to individuate on the financial/vocational level, it was soon obvious to us that Grace needed to separate on the ego/emotional level. Grace was willing to support Peter and to endure his ridicule concerning her conventional, reliable, consistently responsible career traits, as long as Peter did not abandon her.

Because Grace lacked emotional confidence to live without Peter, she allowed him to dominate and manipulate her. She looked the other way to keep the peace, refused to see how irresponsible he was, and acquiesced to what was often Peter's cruel and demeaning behavior during their ten-year relationship.

Peter, on the other hand, was dependent on Grace for financial support. Because he lacked confidence in his own ability to support himself, he defended against his weakness by dominating and manipulating her. He threatened to leave her whenever she complained or tried to get him to take a job. He chastised her for her lack of understanding of his need for creativity and freedom.

Grace finally got the courage to boot Peter out. He was astonished when she gave him the ultimatum of getting and keeping a job of his choice and paying his fair share or leaving. He was also so confident that she did not mean what she said that he moved in with his parents in order to teach Grace a lesson. But Grace had had it with Peter's excuses and financial

But parents do not live forever, nor does deteriorating health always permit them to live without assistance. When the time comes for older children to help elderly parents in need of care, the choices should be objective and the determining factors should be what is best all-round for them. The principle of independence is still effective to the extent possible. For example, instead of relocating the elderly into their children's homes or nursing homes, home health care assistance in their own home offers continued independence in familiar surroundings.

Nursing homes are viable options, especially when infirmities are severe, and for this reason, nursing home insurance can be considered before needed. If the elderly must use their resources to provide for their own nursing home care, then so be it. Inheritances are not the birthright of grown children as much as the right of the elderly to finish their days in dignity and comfort.

There are alternatives for the elderly to live independently, besides being alone, moving into nursing homes, or living with relatives. Families can explore such options as home-health care, visiting nurses, day-care centers for adults, and meals-on-wheels. Each community has its own variations of these programs.

One of the most promising developments are assisted living programs which are largely privately owned and licensed by the state, although some are government subsidized. They offer attractive private residences for couples or individuals with communal dining, housekeeping and personal assistance, nursing and medical staff in-residence or on-call, handicapped facilities and recreational programs, all geared to the needs of the elderly.

We might already be supporting through tax dollars some of these alternatives which can help our own families when the time comes. Since almost half of Americans over age 65 will stay in a nursing home at some time, we need to familiarize ourselves with what they have to offer. Publicly, tax-supported nursing homes, often unjustly criticized for lacking quality, must still adhere to the same federal and state regulations as private nursing homes and often offer the benefit of lower cost, without necessarily compromising quality. It pays to shop around.

Living wills with durable power of attorney help ensure that the wishes of the elderly are followed without the interference of unnecessary or unwanted medical procedures. Living wills allow the elderly to make their own decisions about dying and take the burden off relatives. Many people know and fear the horrors that have occurred because extraordinary medical procedures were taken to sustain life when there was no reasonable hope of recovery. Aside from the exorbitant expense, everyone suffers from the prolonged and often painful death that results.

When Ann, who was 68, came for therapy, she was in a state of depression. Her husband had died several months before. Ann had worked through most of her grief over his death, but she had not worked through the "financial disaster" she now found herself in. She and her husband had been living a rather high style of life, and they both had become accustomed to it.

Unfortunately, after her husband died, she learned that his pension with his company ended. The little life insurance money she received paid for a "first class" funeral and the major outstanding bills. This left Ann with just her social security to live on. The couple had no children or family whom she could depend upon. These circumstances brought on Ann's depression. She envisioned herself in the future as hungry, cold, and in rags.

During therapy, Ann learned to refute the irrational and catastrophic thinking regarding her supposed financial disaster. She began to figure out how to make do with what she had. She sold her heavily mortgaged home and moved to an inexpensive efficiency apartment, took precautions to maintain the car she had, changed her shopping habits without sacrificing tasty, nutritious, but inexpensive food, and she joined a senior citizens group for recreation. All of these changes had previously been beneath Ann, but she surprised herself at how she adjusted, managed, and even began to take pride in her resourcefulness.

Ann's depression lifted and a new sense of independence and confidence took its place. The simple point was that she could (when she had to) get by with a relatively lowered standard of living. She gave up luxuries she had been used to, concentrated on the essentials of living, but resisted the temptation to become a sick person over her change in circumstances. She actually became a happier, more independent, and more fulfilled individual.

How many others like Ann unnecessarily wind up depressed and dependent upon society because they make a catastrophe out of changes in their lives rather than rationally evaluate the situation? What Ann finally did was "act" responsibly rather than merely "react" to the circumstances.

To the elderly who find themselves unable to say no to their older children when they ask for money, we have some recommendations which again reinforce the principles we have already stated for financial independence. This time it is the elderly parent or parents who must recognize that bailing out children in crises, especially when they have a pattern of dependency, can contribute to the problem, not help solve it.

The most important question the elderly parent must answer is whether the older child has the capacity to make a living and support himself or herself and any dependent children. If the elderly parents can't make that determination, they should seek the assistance of social services organizations where they are trained to evaluate crisis situations objectively.

Counseling can take many different forms from intensive psychotherapy to vocational/financial counseling. Whatever is needed can be provided and it could be as straightforward as teaching a displaced homemaker how to stop living beyond her means, discontinue all use of credit cards, and learn to live on a cash basis. When parents merely step in and pay all the bills, or permanently take the children into their own homes, they are not really solving the problem.

What is unfortunate is that so many elderly parents, especially grandparents, are finding themselves raising their grandchildren because their own son or daughter is seen as incompetent. When the situation involves addiction to drugs or alcohol, physical abuse, abandonment, criminal behavior, or imprisonment, grandparents often have little recourse but to parent the grandchildren. Obviously this is also a social problem, but one thing is clear, the emergence of dependency is the related cause which must be addressed when social welfare policy is defined. People have just not achieved adult independence.

What everyone can do as individuals, though, is to give each generation within the family an opportunity for independence while maintaining a mature level of cooperation. Overinvolvement in each other's lives is not the way to accomplish that goal. If one truly understands that independence is achieved by being fully adult in all major areas of life, then all are better able to make the necessary decisions that will foster independence. This can be accomplished without sacrificing the intimacy and commitment that comes from relating to each other on an adult-to-adult basis.

Chapter Five
Handling
Difficult
Situations

Using case histories from actual life situations, this chapter examines how dependency, particularly on the ego/emotional level, affects serious difficulties such as those involving financial crises, relationships, unwanted or unplanned pregnancy, abortion, homosexuality, running away, dropping or failing out of school, job quitting or loss of job, criminal behavior, alcohol and drug abuse, depression and anxiety, suicide threats or attempts, disabling or terminal illnesses, crises at retirement, or inability to cope with the death of a spouse. Keynote here is specific, practical, and tested advice on how to handle each "big trouble" from the perspective of encouraging independence.

Now we come to the area that most people fear—in the process of being "on your own," what if big trouble occurs? Since trouble seen by one person can slip by unnoticed by another, it will be difficult to cover every conceivable situation. Rather, we'll keep the discussion to those areas we have most frequently seen in counseling and therapy.

While fear is often realistic and justifiable, we need to understand the basis for the magnitude of fear. Fear can range from mild, rational, apprehensive, and cautious to intense, irrational, suspicious, deluded, or even paranoid. Fear can also range from concern for others to concern about ourselves.

When the moment of truth comes in counseling with people in "big trouble," time and time again they admit that the underlying problem is **fear**, not anger, guilt, or jealousy. One woman came for help because of the anger and guilt she was experiencing while ending a twenty-five year marriage. At the basis of her pain was the need for her to work through long-standing dependency based upon her fear of abandonment.

In this case, the woman's difficulty was characterized by her blaming others for her problems and blaming herself for theirs. She blamed herself for the troubles of her two daughters, and she blamed her husband for all her problems. One daughter was having serious difficulties in the second year of her marriage, and the other was abusing drugs and alcohol while in college.

It took some time for her to be able to see that her fear for her daughters was based upon her own fear for herself at not being an adequate mother. Only when she accepted her own dependency—because she had never been "on her own" emotionally or egoically—was she able to start becoming more independent. As she became more independent, she was able to let go of the dependency she had fostered between her daughters and herself. This mother had finally taken the first steps necessary to break the vicious cycle of dependency—a cycle which, incidentally, she was perpetuating in her relationship with her daughters.

Too many parents fear big trouble for their grown children because they still feel responsible for them. The question is, "Why do parents feel responsible for grown children?" Often the answer is because they fear failure as parents and ultimately as persons, so they defend themselves through blaming. If they blame others successfully, the problems are someone else's fault; there is nothing they can do about them—they are off the hook. If they blame themselves successfully, they condemn themselves as flawed, worthless, bad, and finally, helpless. Either way, in the end they relinquish responsibility for themselves.

What can a flawed, worthless, bad, and helpless person do about anything? Nothing. Nothing that is except live out their days depressed, suicidal, and miserable. They are off the hook. Rather than face their fears and accept responsibility "on their own," many parents angrily blame others (their children, their spouse, society...), or they blame themselves. Frequently this dangerous pattern of behavior is taught unconsciously by parents to their children, who in turn behave in the same way when they are older and have their own children.

Have any of us ever really met a perfect person? We're hard pressed to think of any. Yet, somehow people torture themselves into thinking that they "should be" perfect parents, perfect spouses, perfect sons or daughters, perfect grandparents. The truth is that everyone makes mistakes, and everyone can learn from their mistakes. That may sound simple enough, but when people are in the thick of a dilemma, often they lose awareness or the ability to respond as functioning adults. Nothing is ever improved by blaming themselves or others. People need to start where they are at the time.

With this understanding, once again we emphasize the theme of this book. The best way to be of service to oneself and others—even when someone is in "big trouble"—is to do everything possible for them, but do nothing they can do for themselves. Also, as much as possible, one needs to allow them to experience the consequences of their own behavior. Having others do for themselves allows them the opportunity to learn from success. Not bailing them out allows them to learn form their mistakes. People learn both ways.

People still can give each other support and understanding without giving or taking away responsibility. Letting individuals be responsible for themselves and letting them experience the consequences of their own behavior is not abandoning children, spouses, friends, or elderly parents. Done gradually and consistently from the very beginning of the relationships, these are the very skills that will enable people to cope in an increasingly demanding, high speed, complex world.

One of the greatest gifts people give to significant others in their lives is confidence in them to make it on their own. When people give someone their confidence along with the chance to experience being on his or her own in an environment that rewards responsibility, all share in the growth.

If people have not been gradually giving up responsibility for others or communicating that message right along, they can start whenever they are aware of the importance of doing so. At whatever point people make this commitment, they start to communicate confidence in the other person, no matter how many times that person fails in the process or doubts their sincerity.

A person who is allowed to experience the negative consequences from getting into trouble has a better chance of eventually waking up to the connection between his or her behavior and the results. This is an essential step in developing "response-ability." When the person does make this connection, he will think twice before repeating the experience. And if not, it can't be helped by those who know the time has come to step aside and let that person grow up. On the other hand, a "bail out" from trouble holds the promise of a repeat performance.

Now let us look at numerous "big trouble" situations and how to deal with each. Keep in mind that the guidelines we give are aimed primarily at facilitating adult independence, which might not immediately solve the whole problem, but certainly will go to the root of the problem.

Financial Crises

By examining this topic in relation to older adolescents and young adults, it is evident that patterns of behavior learned at this stage of life can profoundly influence the way middle-aged and elderly individuals handle financial difficulties. Keep in mind our first principle–that adolescence is protracted when someone has failed to individuate or become independent in any one of the six major areas of development and that includes financial/vocational.

A lack of financial independence may occur because a person's growth has been arrested in some particular area. It is also possible that because someone has skipped over some necessary early developmental task, later when a problem emerges he or she regresses back to adolescent or child behavior.

An example of financial "big trouble" occurs when someone is chronically irresponsible in the payment of bills, such as rent, loan payments, and credit bills, and is subject to denials, evictions, and repossessions. If the person doesn't have enough money to pay the rent, let him or her negotiate with the landlord or face eviction. If someone needs more money, he or she must earn it, borrow it, or move to less expensive housing.

In the process of getting out of debt, the person may have to sell a car or other belongings, or take loans that must be personally paid back later. If dormitory living is less expensive than the previous arrangements, college students can move into dormitories. Giving advice, empathizing, or directing someone to financial services will help sort out the difficulty, but not accepting another person's responsibility for the situation.

Whatever arrangements are made, the important experience gained is that no one is going to bail the person out. He or she is responsible for making whatever arrangements are necessary. Everyone understands clearly and up front where the responsibility lies.

Like so many guidelines, there are no hard and fast rules. Personal circumstances are different and there is room for flexibility. With young people, for example, our strategy where money is concerned is to keep them on the edge—that means always having to reach for that which they can obtain themselves. Parents help financially only when the acquisition of necessary goods or services is impossible for the young person, and only when the parents themselves can afford to help.

If college students are broke, they learn to go without luxury items and non-essentials, such as vacations, trips, the latest clothing, eating out, long distance telephone calls, entertainment, and parties. If they want to have those things, they will have to earn the money to supply them. If parents want to give these items from time to time, they may find that their gifts are more appreciated once young people have experienced the reality of supplying or doing without the items themselves.

When students take out loans with the government or private institutions to attend college, they are responsible for paying them back. The appalling failure rate on the pay-back for college loans is a lesson on what happens when the government plays the role of irresponsible parent, reluctant or unable to enforce the rules of adult responsibility. The pay-back rate went up considerably after the government got tough and students got the message that there would be no escape from their defaulted loans. Delinquent borrowers were tracked down, given bad credit ratings, and subjected to the full extent of the law.

The loss of a good credit rating is strong incentive to pay bills. The only way Americans will stop living beyond their means is to be held accountable for their actions. Bailouts by relatives and well-meaning friends, and the forgiveness frequently afforded by bankruptcy only compound and continue the problem. The majority of people in financial crises got that way because they used credit to overextend their purchasing power. They need to learn how to live on a cash basis first, before they can learn to manage credit. The best time to do this is when they are young.

If people have to learn responsibility by losing a good credit rating, then it is a hard lesson they need to learn. Credit ratings can be re-evaluated much easier than entrenched attitudes of irresponsibility can be reversed. The little lessons associated with obligations, lessons that were not learned early on, lead to harder lessons later in life.

Problems can be avoided by teaching people how to budget for an upcoming school year or first year on the job, and making sure everyone knows what terms, if any, are negotiable. First they learn to list all sources of income including grants, loans, scholarships, personal savings, money from parents and any income expected from a part-time or full-time job. Then they list necessary expenses such as tuition, fees, room and board, books, transportation, insurance, and medical expenses, laundry and toiletries, car upkeep and gas. If the budget is going to work, discretionary spending, such as entertainment, clothes, vacations, trips home, weekend trips and so on should be part of the budget.

At what point on the continuum of learning people finally wake up to their own accountability for themselves often depends upon how consistently the rules they live by are enforced, and most importantly, understood. In some cases, this may never happen, not because it is impossible, but because they never become aware of the cause and effect relationship involved in adult responsibility. This could be the single most important reason why social-financial services are needed to help people in crisis. The critical issue, though, is to ensure that the lessons of personal responsibility are taught at the same time.

When senior citizens plan their budgets for their retirement years, they seldom factor in expenses for bailing out their adult children. More and more consumer credit counseling services are reporting an increase in concern from senior citizens about how to keep their retirement money from being siphoned off by their older children. Stories abound where elderly parents are paying their children's bills or suffering the consequences of having co-signed loans for children who can't pay their own bills.

When older children pressure their parents with pleas for money, the parents should ask themselves if the older child is capable of earning a reasonable living. If not, they should encourage them to change jobs or help them find the appropriate vocational-rehabilitation services that can help correct that situation. If a woman is left with several small children and no skills to earn her own living, there are programs which can provide immediate assistance such as temporary housing, displaced homemakers training programs, and legal, personal, and money management counseling.

When elderly parents pay the bills for older children, they do so not only at a financial hardship, but an emotionally binding one also. They may think they are doing their children a favor, when in fact, they may be encouraging a pattern of learned helplessness that only makes the financial problem worse. Some financial difficulties of the elderly were discussed in the previous chapter.

Relationship Difficulties

This category includes break-ups, marital conflicts, separations, and divorces. For those eighteen years and older, the choice of partner is theirs, and theirs alone, legally and personally. Parents can give unmeddling advice when asked. Meddling advice is rarely followed anyway. Also parents provide the best lessons through example during the contacts of daily living.

Whether people know it or not, whether they want to or not, they communicate the messages others will learn from them in hundreds of ways, using body language, innuendo, and outright exposition. The more aware they are of their own strengths and weaknesses in relationships, the better they can pass on more effective ways of living, rather then just repeat what they learned when they were young.

One case of misguided parental interference in a relationship involved an older couple whose daughter, a college student, took up residence locally with an unemployed man. The parents suspected the man of dealing in drugs. The father became relentlessly critical, and the daughter stopped seeing her parents. The mother, passive and dependent, worried herself sick, but was unable to persuade the father to leave the daughter alone.

The father continued to harass the daughter and threaten the man. This only increased the daughter's resolve to defy her parents, who incidentally, continued to pay her college bills, even though she was failing college through lack of involvement. When she finally broke off the relationship with the man, she immediately moved back home, never doubting her right to do so.

The parents felt they had won her back, but the real dynamics of the situation were never understood. Subsequently, she established a series of relationships with men, moving in and out of unsuccessful living arrangements, and always returning home to parents who felt responsible for her and who continued to pay her expenses when she could not. It wasn't until she was twenty-six and dramatically abandoned in an affair with a married man, that she sought psychological help.

She began to understand her need to become independent from her parents and was able to move far enough from home, both physically and psychologically, so that she could function independently of her well-meaning, meddling parents. The parents never gained any insight into themselves or their own fear of failure as parents and how it fostered dependency. Instead they redirected their attention to other grown children in the family, who were having marital difficulties where dependency also figured into the problems.

Most people know the pain of breaking off a relationship, and have probably either seen that kind of pain or experienced it at least once in their lifetime. "Breaking Up Is Hard To Do," no matter what decade it is, but the pain diminishes with time and understanding. Where young people are concerned, it is actually easier for them if they go through their early disappointments in relationships while they are away from home.

The attentive peer can be a more effective confidant than an overly involved parent who may not have handled those painful experiences very well in the past. Peers may have recently experienced similar feelings or rejections themselves. If a young person comes home grieving over a broken relationship, parents need to be careful not to over-react or under-react. The grief is real and the pain hurts, but let the grieving period be brief—a few days at most. Missing school or work for more than a day or two is strongly discouraged; otherwise, dependency is fostered.

As with all major relationship problems, the best attitude for relatives and close friends is to be supportive, understanding, and accepting, but not take sides. They rarely know the whole story. Often people come for counseling with a story about how terribly their spouse or partner has treated them, complete with shocking details. Through years of experience, counselors know that they need to hear the other side of the story from the other partner, before they can help the couple to sort out the truth of the dilemma. Often the other side is just as shocking!

Relatives and friends usually take sides with their own in a relationship dispute. Relatives and friends rarely have the objectivity to bring about understanding, but they can provide a useful outlet for angry and hurt feelings. By getting anger out, an individual in a relationship crisis may be in a better position to work out the problem through understanding with the partner or spouse, which is the only way the couple can completely resolve their differences.

Normally, relatives and friends will tell individuals in conflict what they want to hear, not necessarily what they need to hear. People undergoing domestic turmoil need to be confronted, or better yet confront themselves, with their role in the demise of a relationship. Only in that way can understanding, acceptance, and trust come about.

These same precautions hold true for older parents whose grown children are involved in marital conflict, separation, or divorce. Parents should encourage the couple to "work it out on their own" using open and honest communication, mutual understanding, acceptance, and trust. If they are stuck, are not communicating openly and honestly, can not obtain any mutual understanding of the difficulties, refuse to accept each other or the reality of the dilemma, and are unable to trust each other, then the couple should seek professional help.

The most common mistake made by parents of any age is to take their sons or daughters back into their home, frequently with their grandchildren, during a separation. Instead of encouraging them to move back to their own home with their spouse and get help with the relationship, the parents wring their hands in despair, foster dependency on parents, and widen the breach between the couple.

When it is easier to separate than it is to work through the interpersonal strife, the tendency is to take the easy way out. Inevitably it leads to greater problems later. Once people dig their heels in and get used to the new arrangement (especially if they have transferred their dependency from a spouse or partner back to their parents), there is no incentive to tackle the tough problems that started the trouble in the first place.

Parents and relatives can not make a commitment for a couple to resolve their differences and continue the relationship. Only the couple can do that. Because parents are biased, their interference may discourage the tentative understanding the couple will need to work out their differences. The parents' home should not be used as a haven to escape ordinary interpersonal strife. In fact, our professional experience is that success is significantly diminished when parents encourage children to move back to the parents' home with relationship problems. With some exceptions, which we will discuss later, even social visits back home should be weekly at most, and rarely are daily visits recommended for couples in trouble.

One young man, married and with three children, visited his parents every day, usually with his wife and children. The wife, married young, had become dependent on her husband and his parents. She had run away from her parents, had gotten pregnant and then married, and had no family of her own nearby. On two occasions in this marriage, the whole family had moved in with the young man's parents.

It was not uncommon for the older parents to provide meals and watch the grandchildren. Although they complained constantly to others about the burden the daughter-in-law and grandchildren were, they never directly addressed the problem with their son or his wife. Assertions attempted were always by innuendo, never direct. The environment was neither healthy nor happy. It is likely the situation would have continued without change, if the son had not developed health problems. An astute physician detected stress as the root cause of the young man's physical problem and suggested psychotherapy.

Because the young father felt he could not handle total responsibility for the marriage and his family, he was depending upon his parents to help him. The parents themselves could not resist being involved in his family, because they feared being "bad parents." The young father had not been conscious of the dynamics in any of these relationships. When he was able to see the problem more clearly, he began to disengage from his parents' influence in his life, starting with fewer daily visits.

The young wife also came for counseling and she learned to assert herself and accept more personal autonomy as a wife, a mother, and a person, in order to move towards separation/individuation, which had not yet occurred. At the same time, she started preparing for her high school equivalency test and that strengthened her self concept. Although the couple had a lot of work to do before this marriage would survive, the real work needed to start on an individual basis.

The time when parents can encourage their children to come home with their troubles is whenever the four "A's" are involved: assault, addiction, adultery, or abandonment. If any of the four "A's" prevail, parents need not hesitate to provide a temporary shelter for the young person.

When assault, addiction, adultery or abandonment are involved, professional help needs to be sought as soon as possible. Family members are not the best ones to counsel. Most communities have some type of crisis center listed in the telephone book which can provide referrals to a service agency or professional for the particular problem. Because of the seriousness of these situations, the best thing parents can do while providing refuge for anyone is to help them get the objective, professional assistance they need. Anything else might actually make the situation worse.

Unwanted/Unplanned Pregnancy

Parents are responsible for providing for their children's education, and that includes sex education. Exactly how they exercise that responsibility is a separate issue. Whether they are taught about sex directly from parents or the schools, someone needs to teach them about safe and fulfilling sex. But too few people systematically are taught anything about sex, let alone safe and fulfilling sex, or their sources of learning frequently are misinformed peers, street information, or media distortions.

Many parents who are aware of the need will educate their own children about sex. But everyone needs access to complete and accurate information about sex and the consequences of sexual activity. Since this is frequently not the case, sexual ignorance in society results in sexually transmitted diseases, unwanted and unplanned pregnancies, and a variety of other sexual difficulties.

We are not going to resolve the complicated issues associated with sex education here, but we can offer some personal
guidelines for parents who accept the basic premise of this
book, that adults are responsible for their own actions, and that
includes their sexual activity. We are, after all, talking about
those aged eighteen and over. Accurate information about sex
allows responsible people to make better choices regarding
their own sexual conduct.

Parents would be wise to let children know before they
become sexually active, just what the parents' position is
regarding sexual responsibility. If parents believe that young
people who engage in sex must assume the consequences, then
they need to communicate the importance of safe and responsible sexual behavior. Even if parents tried to send this message and failed and an unplanned pregnancy results, they must
decide whether they still believe in the position of accountability. The actions of the parents and the individuals involved will
reflect the commitment to adult responsibility.

The important point for all parties involved in dealing
with an unplanned pregnancy is to do so in accordance with
their own values. For example, if the parents do not approve
of abortion, they should not support one for a son or daughter
by helping arrange for it or pay for it. Instead, they can
encourage and assist with an adoption. Likewise, if the older
parents encourage an abortion, but the mother wants to keep the
baby, the older parents are not obliged to bring the baby or the
mother into their home with them. (Abortion will be covered
in more detail in the next section.) Being able to provide for
the child themselves is a key element in whether the expectant
individuals involved can handle the responsibility of parenthood.

Whatever assistance grandparents can and wish to give to
manage pregnancy, birth, and subsequent living conditions
needs to reinforce the idea that responsibility rests solely in the
hands of the expectant couple involved. To those who feel this
is hard advice to follow, we can only emphasize that the harder

and longer course lies ahead for those who refuse to encourage independence.

Karen came to us when she discovered her 20 year-old daughter was pregnant. The only daughter, Trudy, had been living at home since she graduated from high school, worked only part-time, helped very little around the house, and dated men whom Karen regarded as unreliable. Karen's husband had never been involved with child rearing, worked night-shift, and expected Karen to handle this latest crisis with their pregnant daughter.

Trudy had done poorly in high school, had little self-confidence, and no job skills. Because her mother felt sorry for her daughter, she allowed Trudy to get away with things she knew did not encourage independence. She never asserted herself to Trudy about getting a full-time job, moving away from home, and taking care of herself, although she frequently talked to others about the need for this.

Earlier, when Trudy's girlfriend became pregnant and the father left town, her friend's parents allowed the daughter to continue living in their home. The parents assumed responsibility for both mother and child. Trudy saw nothing wrong with this arrangement and fully expected her own mother to be pleased with her pregnancy and do the same for her. Karen felt it was unfair to have a baby in the house with her husband working night-shift, but moreover, she really didn't want to raise her daughter's baby herself.

Karen knew her daughter well enough to know that once the euphoria of being pregnant became the reality of taking care of a baby, Karen would end up doing most of the work. Difficult as it was for her, she knew that unless she asserted herself now, before the baby arrived, things would end up exactly as she predicted. The question was whether Karen had the strength to follow through with the actions that would force Trudy to accept responsibility for herself.

Karen wanted Trudy to have an abortion before it was too late. Trudy was appalled, because she wanted the baby very much. She couldn't understand why her mother was so upset. As expected, the father of the child avoided Trudy, causing her first disillusionment. Karen told Trudy from the start that she would have to move, because they did not want a baby in the house. Trudy knew from experience that if she stalled long enough, her mother would relent.

Karen was determined this time not to fail Trudy by pandering to her fears and manipulations and thereby promoting dependence. With help, Karen located a shelter for unwed mothers willing to accept Trudy. Trudy had consistently refused to go for any help from social service organizations. Karen set a deadline for Trudy to be out of the house and made sure Trudy understood that Karen would take her to the shelter if Trudy could not make other arrangements herself.

When the deadline came, Trudy had no place to go. Filled with resentment and anger, she reluctantly let her mother drive her to the shelter for unwed mothers. Karen never heard from Trudy during the next four months of the pregnancy, but she learned from the shelter that Trudy had a healthy baby boy. Trudy began working at a day care center where she was able to keep her son with her while she worked to support herself and the child. She and the child were living modestly, but on their own.

It was many sad and difficult months for Karen before she heard from Trudy again. With help from the shelter, Trudy was fortunate to receive some counseling for the next six months. For Trudy growing up and accepting responsibility for herself was very traumatic and painful.

Because she had counseling throughout the process, Karen was able to avoid blaming herself for her daughter's predicament. In this particular case, a reconciliation between Karen and Trudy did eventually occur about a year later. But it could easily have gone the other way. Although she may have never seen her parents again, Trudy could have remained attached to them through her anger and resentment for the rest of her life.

In this particular case, though, Trudy grew up, also. She survived breaking away from her parents, and finally became responsible for herself. When Trudy and her mother were reconciled, they experienced a relationship between two adults for the first time in their lives together.

It is unfortunate for many parent-child relationships that the process of separation does not occur earlier. Parents and children have numerous opportunities over the years to experience what we call successful mini-separations. When this happens, both parents and older adolescents move more easily into the stage of mature relationships.

Abortion

It may seem inappropriate to include abortion among the many difficult and troublesome situations we have been discussing. We do this not because abortion is a difficult or troublesome situation in and of itself, because surely that is not always the case. There are many women, men, and families who go through the process of abortion without difficulty or trouble. We would have to be naive to assume, however, that that is always the case. Difficulties abound intra-personally and interpersonally not because of abortion "per se," but because of the way people look at or perceive abortion.

For our purposes here, whether abortion is right or wrong or whether abortion should be legal or illegal are moot questions. There is no empirical or observable evidence to show that "human" life begins at conception, birth, or somewhere in-between. We simply do not know.

The difficulties we want to address result from the different perceptions people have about abortion. As the ancient adage goes, "People are not really disturbed by other people, situations, and things, but by the way they look at other people, situations, and things." And one thing is certain—abortion is looked upon differently by different people.

Some ways of handling difficulties that can arise because of differing perceptions of abortion are more effective than others. Parents and a child, eighteen or older, can disagree on what action to take regarding an unwanted pregnancy: abortion or no abortion. One case discussed the issue of abortion briefly in the previous section regarding unplanned or unwanted pregnancy. There we saw that acting in accordance with one's own values and assuming full responsibility for the outcome of the actions was the principle to follow. Assuming this is accomplished, the difficulties often continue because different perceptions of abortion result in a breakdown of communications, failure to understand, refusal to accept, and lack of trust.

Communications need to continue openly and honestly. Someone needs to have the courage to initiate the dialogue about abortion, as awkward as it might seem. This is not the time to withdraw. Something said is better than nothing said even if it is said with anger. Blowing off steam might be necessary. An objective friend or counselor is frequently a big help with this process. Keep talking.

Listening—really listening—facilitates understanding. People who are really listening to each other do their best to try to see the situation as the other person does, rather than color it with their own perceptions. They are looking at a situation through red glasses and someone else is looking at it through green glasses. What they need to try is to see it through the green glasses also. Even if they don't like green, they will be able to see it the way someone else does and that is understanding. They also need to watch how the messages they send are not always the messages the other person receives and vice versa.

Acceptance means people recognize and understand what another has said or done without necessarily agreeing with it. Reality is what is and acceptance of reality is sanity. Denial and withdrawal from reality is insanity. When people link agreement or liking with acceptance they create a major obstacle for themselves and others. When someone asked Mother Theresa of Calcutta how she was able to tolerate so well the appalling human suffering and poverty she saw for so long, she replied in three words... "accept, accept, accept." She often did not like what she saw and responded when she didn't, but she did accept.

Acceptance creates an atmosphere of freedom in which people can be themselves and share their inner world of meaning and feeling. Effective counselors and therapists know this and that is why they refrain from judgement. They unconditionally regard or accept what they hear. By being themselves and being honest, effective counselors and therapists encourage their clients to do likewise. Thus trust is established and the relationship is characterized by depth and growth. The ability to trust another is determined by the ability to trust oneself. People who take risks, let go and are themselves, give others the chance to do the same.

Barbara left home at nineteen and moved out west. She became involved with a man who she later found out was addicted to drugs, prone to infidelity, and dependent on her and welfare checks for financial survival. Not practicing safe and responsible sex, Barbara became pregnant by the man whom she now regarded as a very poor candidate for husband and father. Because Barbara had been brought up in a family opposed to abortion, she struggled with the decision to have one, but then did so rather quickly.

At the time of the abortion, Barbara also terminated the relationship with the man and returned home. After having second thoughts about her decision regarding the abortion, she went through a very painful period of remorse and grieving. Finally Barbara was able to accept that what she had done was all that she could have done under the circumstances. The fact that she now thought differently ("I could have had the baby and arranged for adoption") had nothing to do with her decision at the time of the abortion. She took what she thought to be the right action and at the time she thought it was OK. By not judging her past action by present outcome, she was able to accept not only the action but also herself.

Since Barbara had always had an open and honest relationship with her parents, she did not resist telling them what she had done. The parents listened with shock and disbelief, but they continued to listen. Both parents spoke in anger and voiced their own values while Barbara listened—really listened. Her parents would never agree with what she had done. They disliked the fact that Barbara had had an abortion but admitted they could understand why she had done it. The parents genuinely appreciated the fact that their daughter trusted them enough to tell them what had happened. Barbara and her parents finally, as independent adults, agreed to disagree. They did so through open and honest communications, mutual understanding, acceptance, and trust. Their relationship continued to retain those characteristics.

Homosexuality

As with abortion, homosexuality is not included in this chapter because it is a difficulty in and of itself. There are many homosexuals who experience little or no difficulty with their orientation. We include homosexuality here because of the different ways it is looked upon by different people—ways which result in broken communications, misunderstanding, rejection, and mistrust.

Once again the outcome of the failure to deal with differing perceptions is our focus and not whether homosexuality is "inherited" or "learned," "predetermined" or "chosen." The results of scientific research on the origins of homosexuality, much like that of "human life" or even intelligence, still leaves the issue of homosexuality a moot point. We simply do not know with any significance when and to what extent homosexuality is caused by genetics and/or environment. Even if there were significant evidence, difficulties among people would persist because people often ignore objective scientific data. For example, millions of people start or continue to smoke despite clear evidence that smoking is injurious to health and can be fatal.

Equally moot is whether homosexuality is a chosen or predetermined sexual orientation. Whether in fact people ever freely and totally "choose" any behavior, or anything for that matter, is a question which has been debated perennially without conclusion by the most erudite philosophers. Perhaps freedom of choice comes with full awareness or enlightenment and from that moment on there are no choices to be made, only spontaneous natural action.

The only conclusion we can draw with certainty at this point with regard to the source and course of homosexuality is that different perceptions have resulted in difficulties. These difficulties exist and are likely to continue to exist for some time. As with abortion, nothing has been proven conclusively and if people do not agree perceptually, then they can still communicate, understand, accept, and trust.

In all our years of working with people in counseling and therapy, we have yet to meet parents who intentionally raised their son or daughter to be homosexual. Quite the opposite, parents are usually unduly upset when their son or daughter announces or presents a homosexual orientation. As a result, understanding is blurred, acceptance diminished, relationships are strained, and both the young adult and the parents suffer.

Earlier we discussed six major areas where maturation must occur in order for an older adolescent to become an adult. Growing up sexually is part of the physical independence that needs to take place. But being sexually independent involves more than just being able to function sexually. Sexual independence has wide social, moral, and psychological implications. It involves being responsible for one's own sexual behavior. With the right to engage in sex activity comes responsibility for the outcome of the action. Whether homosexual, bisexual, or heterosexual, that responsibility remains.

In today's society, a gay or lesbian adult needs to be able to respond to social pressure and rejection that comes inevitably with a homosexual orientation. While it is true that many homosexuals have little or no problem with socialization, many do. That discrimination exists as it does today is the reality that gay and lesbian people confront frequently, if not daily. Not being able to handle the social pressure to conform to the heterosexual norm, or effectively respond to or ignore rejection from intolerant people means the homosexual has not yet accepted reality. He or she is holding on to the idea of how life "should be," rather than how it is.

Parents need to understand that whatever the sexual orientation of their son or daughter, their own peace of mind will come with acceptance. Tortured parental self-doubt reveals itself in questions such as, "Where did we go wrong?" or, "Was I a bad role model or parent?" This kind of thinking indicates that the parents themselves are not letting go of their son or daughter or accepting what is.

They also need to accept that as parents they did the best they could (not "perfect") at the time when their child was growing up. Whether they could have done things differently is really quite irrelevant today. They could only act in the moment at hand. The past is just that—past. At the time most parents thought what they were doing for their children was the right thing, or they did not really think about what they were doing at all. In either case, parents of grown children who announce or present a homosexual orientation must make peace with themselves first, even if things didn't turn out the way they wanted or expected.

For example, one of the basic premises of our counseling has always been that we don't judge well-intentioned interventions by the outcomes. We can only choose the actions we take; the outcomes are out of our hands. Whether or not someone changes depends on numerous factors—such as motivation, actions of others, unforeseen circumstances or fate—which are out of our hands.

In this way, people are relieved of the unrealistic desire to control others and outcomes, which are beyond their ability to control anyway. They can accept others and the outcomes. They may not like the behavior of others or the outcomes, and the fact that a situation did not work out as they wanted does not make the actions wrong.

Parents who want to facilitate an adult relationship with a son or daughter who assumes a homosexual orientation must begin by accepting the behavior. We repeat what we have said before: acceptance does not mean we like the behavior or that we agree with the behavior. Acceptance means we recognize the behavior for what it is, someone else's orientation and someone else's responsibility.

Parents can be supportive and communicate that they love their son or daughter without liking or agreeing with homosexuality. Parents can state their feelings about homosexual behavior without rejecting the child. What they need to avoid is brow-beating, putting down, rejecting, or trying to interfere with homosexuality as someone else's orientation.

If the young persons are experimenting with homosexuality because they need to work it through and find out for themselves, parents help most by keeping communication channels open, trying to understand, and being accepting. Whether the person works through homosexuality or not, relatives and friends can still accept them by accepting what is... and what is, simply, is.

One important and helpful thing that people can do for relatives or friends who are gay or lesbian is to encourage them to accept themselves. If people are going to adopt a homosexual orientation, they need to do so with self-honesty, self-understanding, and self-acceptance. If they have not accepted themselves as they are, it is unlikely that they can function as independent adults. Instead they remain arrested as child-adolescents who are defensively and destructively rebelling and fanatically demanding that others and all agree with them. In this regard, homosexuals can be just as bigoted and fanatical as heterosexuals. A fanatic is not an adult.

To repress any sexual desire without self-acceptance and awareness is doomed to create inhibition and frustration, and ultimately will result in failure. To indulge sexual desires without self-awareness and acceptance leads to promiscuity and sexual addiction and is doomed to fail also. Both sexual repression and sexual indulgence without self-acceptance and awareness can lead to sexual dysfunction or sexually deviant behaviors. The key to healthy sexuality is awareness and acceptance of oneself as he or she is, not necessarily as some-one else wants him or her to be. It is really understanding and acceptance that people need from others, not necessarily agreement.

Homosexuals also need to accept when others do not like or agree with homosexuality. For example, a gay or lesbian who brings a special friend home for a visit should not expect to share the same bed when it is against the parents' values. The gesture may be more symbolic than anything else, but it can be a legitimate assertion on the part of the parents. It is also not discriminatory; the same might apply if they were unmarried heterosexuals.

Many times we have seen parents and older adult children who are homosexuals bridge their differences over time through acceptance of the differences. Knowing that it is OK to disagree and even dislike each other's behaviors, without re-jecting the other person as a human being, goes a long way towards this end. Many parents after some time grow so accustomed to the gay or lesbian orientation of one of their children, that they can truly enjoy each other's company on a regular basis. It can happen, but then again even after sincere effort it may not, and perhaps that can't be helped.

Allen came from a close knit family that genuinely en-joyed each other's company. The family spent weekends, holidays, and vacations together. In his late twenties, after several unsuccessful heterosexual relationships, Allen met a gay man with whom he developed an intimate relationship. He felt an attraction toward his male friend that he had never felt for a female. After a few years of struggling with his own thoughts and feelings, Allen finally let go and moved in with his friend in what was to become a committed relationship.

Being the first and only gay or lesbian person in his family, Allen knew that some rough adjustments would have to be made and he was right. Allen was the only son of a "good old boy," and his father took the situation quite hard. His father, a man of strong convictions and opinions, was also a rugged individualist used to taking what he did not like "on the chin" without flinching. His father's philosophy had been that he lived in a free country and he could do anything he wanted as long as it did not interfere with another man's rights. The father had brought up Allen the same way and in this sense they understood and accepted each other without much being said.

Allen's father did not like homosexuality and he thought it was unnatural. As far as he was concerned, he would never agree otherwise. Allen knew and accepted this in his father while his father accepted that Allen's life was his own and Allen was responsible for it. Neither father or son felt the need to resort to the use of power to win at the expense of the other losing.

Allen's mother and three sisters, on the other hand, responded with tears and arguments. However, being a family that did not sweep issues under the carpet, they all continued not only to talk but also to spend time with each other. The women were more concerned about the social ramifications of Allen being homosexual. Their rather jaundiced and limited view of the "gay life-style" turned out to be erroneous after Allen and his partner joined the family on several of their outings. Allen's partner, blessed with a caring, easy-going manner and a quick sense of humor, in time became a welcome addition to the family. The partner's interest in sports was particularly appreciated by Allen's father, an interest not shared by Allen, the mother, or sisters. All in all everyone truly enjoyed each other's company.

The family did not agree and did not pressure each other into agreement regarding homosexuality. Allen and his partner were careful not to unduly offend the family by sleeping together when at their homes or by openly displaying physical

affection. Allen's family, in the same way, did not offend
Allen and his partner by expecting them to sleep apart when
staying with them in their home. This arrangement was
everyone's way of saying they continued to agree to disagree.
For them, it was the way independent adults behaved. Adults
do not necessarily have to agree—they just accept.

Running Away or Moving Out

There's no doubt about it, running away, moving out, or
abandonment of relationship is dramatic. When it happens, it
has an effect on those who remain at home, as well as those who
leave home. But, it happens frequently.

First, we need to distinguish between running away,
moving out, and abandoning a relationship with parents, partners, or elderly parents. When a person leaves home
unannounced and unexpectedly for a brief period of time and
then returns, we regard the incident as running away. If they
set up a relatively permanent living arrangement, either announced or not, we say they have moved out. When the person
breaks off communications with those left behind, either completely or nearly so, and establishes separate living arrangements, we refer to the situation as abandonment of the relationship.

More often than not, the motivation for leaving or the
despair of those left behind is hidden below the surface. Caught
up in the emotional reactions to the situation, those who leave
and those left behind are simply unaware of the underlying
causes. It is normal and natural that the people left at home will
experience disappointment, frustration, or regret when their
son, daughter, spouse, or parent leaves home under trying
circumstances. But to experience intense guilt that is based
upon low self-esteem or depression that is based upon
unexpressed, unresolved anger is unhealthy and unnatural.

When this is the case, those left at home need to work on
themselves, and if necessary, get professional help to sort out
the problems. They can only be an inspiration as adults when

they handle the existing circumstances as adults. It is unrealistic to think adults never make mistakes, or that they did not make mistakes in the past. How they handle their mistakes (whenever they were made) can inspire others to grow in awareness and understanding along with them.

When people leave home, they do so with their own very personal feelings and stories. Basically, they either want to escape perceived or real abusive circumstances in the home, or they need to separate physically from their parents in order to declare their own independence. Consciously or not, they are seeking what we call separation-individuation. The desire to get out of truly abusive circumstances in the home is healthy, and running away could be a genuinely assertive response. We can only hope that the person adjusts and makes a clean break from parents or partners who do not have enough awareness to stop themselves from hurting others. The ignorance is usually so thick when abusive conditions exist in the home, that those who escape need to protect themselves by staying away.

For the abused, the most important tasks are becoming independent, understanding, and (yes), finally forgiving towards the parents or partners. Forgiveness may not necessarily happen directly between the parties involved, but rather occurs within the person who had been abused. It is important that the person understands that forgiving is not liking the abuse or the abuser, but simply deciding to let go of resentment. Difficult as this may be, the road map in life contains some unpleasant trips that can not be avoided. The sooner the abused person can let go of attachment and resentment for the frightening past, the sooner he or she can move into complete adult independence.

On the other hand, the home circumstances could be difficult and trying, but not intolerable. Parents, partners, and the elderly are not perfect. People make mistakes. There is no how-to manual or course to pass before becoming parents or spouses. Leaving home because of perceived intolerable conditions could very well be an attempt to manipulate parents or partners through threat. These individuals may have been conditioned to get what they want in this way through years of reinforcement.

If someone gives in to another's threat of running away, it may reinforce manipulative behavior. Not giving in to the threat may come as a shock to the person running away, especially if the technique of manipulating others was used in the past. But it could be the shock that makes the difference eventually between a healthy individual or a dependent personality. In the following simple case, parents made it clear to their daughter that failure to come home in defiance of them would carry its own consequences.

The daughter ran away from home one evening in a huff because she wasn't allowed to use the car on a school night. She telephoned home from a friend's house and said that she would come home only if she was allowed to use the car, since she thought it was a reasonable request. The parents informed her that they would not respond to threats. They told her that the decision regarding her use of the family car on school nights had already been discussed. If she chose to stay away, that was her choice and responsibility. Using the car was not negotiable. She came home pouting, but she came home. In this way, the parents were able to nip manipulative behavior before the threats became more defiant at another time.

A certain amount of adolescent rebellion is normal, natural, and healthy. Without it, the experience needed for a person to accomplish separation-individuation will not be available. There can be no adults without separation. Running away, moving out, and even abandonment of relationship could be, and frequently are, signs of necessary rebellion. Because of the circumstances that shape each family with its own unique characteristics and stories, leaving home under trying conditions may be the only way someone can grow up.

People need to understand that parents and grown children have many kinds of relationships. How often people see each other is not the test of a good relationship. Some see each other regularly, even daily, while others see each other very infrequently. Although everyone chooses friends and partners, no one chooses children or parents. When parents and children relate to each other as adults, they will see each other because they want to, not because they have to.

When someone sees a dear friend who hasn't been seen for a long time, the length of time between visits does not inhibit deep feelings for that friend. The years seem to evaporate, as both parties openly and eagerly share themselves with each other. The same can apply to parents and their adult children who cut through the defenses that have tied them up in knots of resentment for years.

Many people threaten to leave home motivated by unhealthy fears. Because they lack honesty, understanding, acceptance, trust, or confidence in themselves, they really fear being on their own. They defend against the fear of being on their own by making threats which manipulate parents or partners.

In this ultimately self-defeating way, they are able to keep their parents and partners connected to them. They are, in effect, dependent on the very people they condemn for making their lives miserable. There are plenty of dependent people who continue with this destructive pattern. The anger they exhibit when they threaten to leave home is really motivated by their own fear.

Guilt and resentment in those who remain at home after someone leaves is also based in fear—fear of being inadequate or being a failure. In their minds, they can't let go of their children or spouse. Because they still feel responsible for them, the dependency continues from their side. The guilt they experience is motivated by their own fear, and they resent their children or spouse for making them feel guilty. A vicious cycle.

Parents and partners who have been left, or children who leave home under strained circumstances, need to recognize that the separation and pain could go on for years. The best course of action for those who want a reconciliation is to keep the lines of communication open, as much as possible. They can let the estranged party know occasionally (not constantly) that they are available and willing to talk. If they can extend this invitation periodically and then back off, they give it a better chance of being accepted.

They do not plead with those who have left to come home, nor do they avoid reasonable requests or assertions. They make no unnecessary dramatic gestures, such as calling the police, having friends or relatives intervene, or making long trips to find them. If evidence exists for bona fide emergencies which are truly life-threatening, then assistance from such sources as the police, a dormitory or shelter director, or a crisis center can be sought. If they are unable to communicate meaningfully, a counselor or a mediator who is acceptable to all might help.

While we encourage the people involved to make peace, we want to emphasize that those who were left at home can only extend the invitation; they can't force it. At the heart of any reconciliation and the peace it brings is forgiveness. What we do not mean by forgiveness is merely apologizing, or agreeing with what the person does or has done, or "kissing their boots," or becoming friends and spending lots of time together. Nor does forgiveness necessarily occur when the person who left home in anger, suddenly returns home to live again. Forgiveness simply means letting go of resentment.

The process of forgiving another follows a pattern. First people recognize and accept that they really don't want to forgive the other person. At this point, they cannot want to forgive. Once they have been honest enough to admit this and drop the guilt for not wanting to forgive the other person, then they have taken the first big step. People begin by forgiving themselves for not wanting to forgive.

Next they need to understand what unforgiveness is doing to the other person and to themselves. They become aware of the tension, irritability, high blood pressure, bad moods, indigestion, insomnia, or other symptoms they experience. Finally, while they cannot want to forgive the other person, they can "will" or decide to forgive the other person. Forgiveness is an act of will not of want. The decision is made internally in an instant of time. Amazingly enough, once this is done, the "how to do," the actual forgiving takes care of itself. Once they "will" or make the decision to forgive, how they do it comes rather spontaneously because forgiving is in accordance with nature.

Dropping Out or Failing Out

People who think they can make someone who is eighteen years or older stay in school, study, or get good grades are headed for resentment or disappointment. Individuals who allow themselves to be subjected to this kind of coercion are usually dependent and headed for their own version of resentment or disappointment. Those who use punishment to effect these ends will quickly learn that coercion really doesn't work.

The only potentially worthwhile course is to try to encourage and advise others with realistic appreciation and understanding for what schooling can and cannot do for them. Many people might be far happier and more self-satisfied as manual workers, for instance, than college graduates. Parents and partners who truly accept this and are not just giving it lip service are not likely to use their children's achievements or their partner's accomplishments to puff up their own egos. When they push someone to obtain more and more education to improve job prospects or career goals at the expense of the individual's own aptitudes, needs or preferences, the groundwork is being laid for job dissatisfaction and interpersonal resentment.

The best time to teach children about the advantages of schooling is when they are in high school, and even younger. The best lesson to teach them is that they are responsible for their own learning behavior and the consequences of that behavior. Whether or not those over eighteen decide to stay in school and/or get good grades is their responsibility. The sooner parents realize their life-ambitions for their children are separate from their children's, the better off everyone will be.

When parents allow their children who have dropped out or failed out of school to live at home without a job or without paying for room and board, they are asking for trouble. Grown children need to understand that they must fend for themselves, or they are not welcome to live with their parents. This may sound tough and hard line, but it is necessary.

There are so many case examples that fit into this category, but the one that inspires us the most involved a young woman who dropped out of college during her freshman year. Intense pressure from her parents to go back to college accompanied by her doing nothing while at home produced a nagging sense of unfulfillment and she ran away from home to become a rock musician. Her distraught parents were advised to let go of their own ambitions for her, make it clear that she was on her own, but also encourage her to pursue her career as a musician, which she was determined to do anyway. Difficult as it was for the parents, they stood back knowing vaguely that their daughter's life-style went against most of the values they held.

The young woman was talented enough to support herself for many years in the music business. Finally she decided she was ready to try something else. She put herself through a pre-professional program at a competitive college and graduated with honors; then she went on to get her professional degree. She did it her way, and with no regrets.

The main point here is not to be intimidated or threatened by another's decision to drop out of school or by behavior which results in their failing out. If they are to be on their own, they need to experience the consequences of their behavior.

Criminal Behavior: Arrests, Convictions, Imprisonment

Just as we have repeatedly emphasized the need to accept the consequences for our own behavior, once again we remind readers that those involved in criminal behavior need to experience the consequences of their own behavior. Difficult as it may be to stand by and see a son, daughter, or significant other convicted or sent to prison, everyone must understand that repeatedly bailing out the offender is tantamount to reinforcement of criminal behavior. Bailing them out might include such rescue activities as posting bonds, paying their legal expenses, lying in their behalf, or pulling strings to help them escape legal proceedings and punishment.

The only exception we would make is for first-time offenders who exhibit a genuine desire to straighten themselves out. If they engage in appropriate behavior, seek rehabilitation, and cooperate, then family or friends can help them. In no case do we recommend breaking laws to help criminal offenders. The system may not always be fair, but it is the one everyone must live by.

A case involving Gene, a twenty-four year-old with a history of drug dealing, receiving stolen merchandise, running illegal gambling operations, and check forgery may help illustrate our approach. Gene was arrested numerous times. Each time, his father hired high-priced lawyers and pulled strings to bail Gene out of his troubles. Two convictions resulted in heavy fines and stayed sentences with probation. Gene never had to go to jail, thanks to his father's intervention. The problem was compounded by one divorce and a current marital separation involving two small children. Gene's parents had assumed financial support for the grandchildren and provided significant caregiving for them also. Gene was living at home.

We got involved in this case when Gene's father came to see us. Gene had once again been arrested for peddling stolen merchandise. His father, well known in the area for his own questionable business dealings, was at his wit's end. All he knew for certain was that he wanted to help his son. We reviewed many of the concepts in this book with him, and finally convinced him that it was worth "the gamble" to let Gene experience the consequences of his own behavior—no bail outs, lawyers, or influence. Gambling man that he was, Gene's father was ready to give it a try.

Gene was sent to a medium security prison for four months. As far as we know, it was the first and last time. Following his release, he came for therapy as a ready-to-recover, self-proclaimed "sociopath." Sociopaths are unable to see a causal relationship between their behavior and its manifest results so they fail to profit from learning. Gene was not a sociopath because he had learned.

Gene had enough insight into himself to want to know why he impulsively engaged in criminal behavior. In time he was able to understand his behavior as a defense against anxiety of being on his own emotionally and egoically. Gene's recovery allowed him to reconcile his relationship with his current wife, and he avoided any more arrests and criminal behavior. Gene established himself in his own business, albeit with his father's help, and in this case even we condoned the assistance.

As an interesting side note, Gene's father continued in therapy. During the course of the father's exploration, he admitted in confidence that he felt guilty and hypocritical at not having been a good role model for his son. Acting on his own insight into his role in the dilemma with his son, the father took the initiative to "clean up his own act" in his business dealings. The father very much saw his son's struggle to become more responsible as a second chance for him to do likewise.

Alcohol and Drug Abuse

One of the most important things that parents, relatives, or friends of a drug or alcohol abuser must learn is to stop blaming themselves for the problem. At Al-Anon, a support group for the significant people in the lives of substance abusers, the first lesson learned by those who share the lives of abusers is that they did not cause the problem, nor are they responsible for solving it.

When parents, spouses, relatives, or friends blame themselves for others' substance abuse, they communicate their own responsibility for the problem to the substance abusers. In effect, the abusers can take themselves off the hook or shirk responsibility for themselves. This does nothing more than decrease the likelihood that they will take responsible action in their own behalf. In essence, it increases dependency on the drugs or alcohol, and makes the problem worse, not better.

Before substance abusers will do anything about an alcohol or drug problem, they must admit that there is a problem. For many this means finally having to deal with the results of their own behavior. Remember our basic premise is to allow them as much as possible to experience the consequences of their own behavior. This could mean arrest for drunken driving, drug possession, or other related crimes. It could also mean the loss of a relationship, job, college standing, money, or the diagnosis of serious alcohol or drug related diseases.

No, we do not mean that friends and relatives stand by silently until a disaster such as an automobile accident happens. Every effort is made to alert substance abusers to where their dangerous dependency is leading. Advise them of the alternatives. Give them the names of agencies or programs where they can get help for themselves. Forbid them to use the family car. Do not give them money. If family or friends can afford to provide money for counseling or rehabilitation, offer to help in the same way as for education. If the providers of the illegal drugs to the substance abuser are known, inform the police. But do not do bail them out, support the habit, or permit them to engage in the addiction in the home or presence of family or friends. If parents or spouses are providing an allowance or extra cash that permits the drug habit, then they need to withdraw the allowance.

Take the right action as responsible people, but the results are out of one's hands. Understand that many people must experience the worst, before they will do anything for themselves about an alcohol or drug problem. Understand that ultimately, they alone are the only ones who can solve their problem.

People need to realize that the use of alcohol and drugs is big business. These substances are pictured in the media as glamorous ways to enhance a good time. Many parents are unaware of the powerful messages they send their children with their own daily use of alcohol, nicotine, and over-the-counter drugs.

The best advice to parents or friends trying to help someone who is abusing drugs or alcohol is confidentially to refer them to a professional alcohol or drug therapist or counselor. Also, the sooner the person gets into a reputable, recognized rehabilitation program or group, the better are the chances of recovery.

It is best for relatives not to try dealing with the problem entirely by themselves, even if they are experienced in the field of alcohol or drug rehabilitation. Their efforts might complicate the situation when the person needs to be honest. Their presence could be intimidating. Also, it is typical during alcohol and drug rehabilitation for the abuser to blame someone in the process of getting better, and if that someone is a parent or spouse, the parent or spouse might transfer their anger or guilt onto the substance abuser. It is better for the vulnerable person not to have to handle interpersonal complications involving relatives and spouses directly.

Perhaps drug abusers can't be persuaded to want to go for help, but they might be persuaded to at least see what help can offer. Be sensitive to their confusion and realize that they are actually denying or are afraid of what is happening. If substance abusers are not willing to seek assistance, and the best advice has already been given, then withdraw any support of the habit, and let them go. The worst might have to happen before healing occurs. Relatives and friends can not help someone who does not want to be helped. They can not counsel someone who does not want to be counseled. They must continually remind themselves: "We did the best we could, and that is all we could do, and it is OK, **no matter how it turns out.**"

The following story illustrates some of the principles we have been discussing. Denise came for counseling with long-standing guilt regarding her daughter. Denise was 36 at the time, had never been married, and had been abandoned at the time of her pregnancy by the baby's father. Her daughter Jan, now nineteen years old, was a sophomore in college. Denise paid all Jan's bills, her tuition, room and board expenses, and provided Jan with a sizable allowance. Occasionally, Jan worked at odd jobs, but with no consistency or significant income.

Jan was sexually promiscuous. She frequently brought different male friends home and slept with them. Jan hadn't asked her mother how she felt about these sexual encounters in the home, and certainly, Jan had not asked for permission. Although Denise disapproved and felt this was behavior she did not value, Denise allowed it to occur time and time again, without saying anything to her daughter.

Jan used alcohol and marijuana daily while at college. She also used cocaine occasionally. Before long, Jan failed out of college and moved back home with her mother. Jan was not working and relied entirely upon her mother to provide her with money and pay her expenses. She continued to use drugs and alcohol daily, but Denise forbade Jan to do so at home. Jan absolutely refused to go for help.

It was at this point that Denise came for counseling full of despair for her daughter and confused about how she should handle the situation. For a start, we advised her to immediately cut her daughter's allowance which Jan was using to buy drugs. We also explained why it was important for Denise to insist that Jan get a job and pay her mother something towards room and board expenses at home. If Jan refused, Denise was to ask her daughter to find another place to live. We provided Denise with information about drug addiction and rehabilitation programs in the area, but it took two months to convince Denise that she needed to take some critical action if Jan was going to have a chance to change. Finally, she began to set some boundaries.

Jan refused to work or pay for any of her room and board expenses. Denise asked her to leave and gave her a deadline to either comply or go. Almost immediately after Jan understood her mother was serious and fully intended what she said, Jan was arrested for drunken and disorderly conduct and the possession of marijuana. This could have been interpreted as a plea for help, punishment of her mother, or not facing her own fears of being on her own.

Denise called us in a panic and was ready to provide bail and bring her daughter home. We advised her to let Jan stay in jail and face her own charges the next day. Jan spent one terrifying night in what was, fortunately, a safe, clean facility. For the first time in her life, she knew her mother really meant business and fully intended to follow through on the things she had been telling her.

Jan voluntarily entered a one-month treatment program for substance abusers. Subsequently, she participated in group counseling. Her mother continued in therapy and worked towards understanding her own dependencies and fears. Six months after the incident and confinement in jail, Jan was back in college. She has remained drug free and is well on her way to independent adulthood. So is her mother.

Not all stories have a happy ending, and there is no one way for solving all the crises that periodically arise in life. What we do know for certain, though, is that parents, partners, and children must stop torturing themselves with guilt and fear. After all the reasonable measures to help substance abusers have been taken, they can only step back and accept what they cannot change.

It is never too late for people to understand themselves, but it may be too late for them to make a critical difference in someone else's life when substance abuse is involved. If they pay attention to what is happening within themselves, they will be better able to seize that moment and make that difference. There never were or never will be any guarantees.

Mental Health Problems

There is a vast array of mental health problems that people can experience. Some of these, such as personality disorders, alcohol and drug problems, and adjustment disorders have been discussed earlier in this book. We will now discuss in some detail psychoses, depression, and suicide, including threats, attempts, and completions. There are numerous other serious disorders which we will not cover, such as panic, phobias, obsessive compulsive behavior, eating disorders, and sexual deviation, but the general guidelines discussed can help with these other disorders as well.

Before we go any further, we emphasize that referral to the appropriate professional, such as a psychologist or psychiatrist, is the most important action to be taken. The kinds of mental health problems listed here are best handled by professionals. Understanding of the causes and treatment of mental health problems has improved significantly, and treatment has become much more accessible for practically everyone.

People who are ill or in pain would most likely try to treat the problem with a home remedy first. If that treatment was unsuccessful and the problem persisted or got worse, they would not think twice before seeking medical attention. The same should be true for psychological or mental health problems. Those who are experiencing mental health difficulties, after attempting to help themselves, should get help from mental health professionals. They need not be ashamed.

Attempting to counsel or do therapy with an immediate family member can be an exercise in futility. Most professional therapists and counselors would not attempt to treat their own family members because of the complex interpersonal involvement and the subjective nature of the way family members view and respond to each other. Therefore, make the appropriate referral, and then, if necessary, the whole family can get involved in a directed, healing process.

People need to be sharply aware of the necessity to make referrals to appropriate professionals or agencies when the circumstances warrant. Without exception, we believe every family has had its own share of mental health difficulties. In the course of dealing with mental health problems, people need to remind themselves continually that the best referral is self-referral.

As with all "big trouble" we have discussed, progress begins when people stop blaming. That means they do not blame themselves or others for the problem. Any counseling or therapy program worth the effort will inevitably bring those involved around to this point. Individuals need to assume responsibility for their own lives, and that starts when they get off the blaming cycle.

We will now identify some mental health problems when referral to a professional individual or agency is appropriate.

Psychosis—People who suffer from psychosis lose contact with reality and themselves. Their behavior can be disoriented regarding who they are, where they are, or the time in which they are living. They may hallucinate which means they experience sights, sounds, voices, touches, tastes, or smells that are not experienced by anyone else present.

When an individual hallucinates, he is fully identified with and believes in what is taking place. If someone questions or refutes the experiences a psychotic person is having, he usually responds with confusion, disbelief, and resistance. For example, a person claims that he hears or sees angels singing, but he can not understand or accept that no one else hears or sees them.

Another sign of psychosis is delusions which can be bizarre, such as delusions of persecution or grandeur. Without the slightest recognition that the delusions are coming from fear, a person might believe she is being punished or sought out, without any basis in fact. For example, the person might suspect that police or CIA agents are following her around day and night, watching every move she makes. The suggestion that this is unwarranted or unlikely is met with disbelief or hostility. In the case of delusions of grandeur, someone claims that she is an important world figure or queen, without any recognition to the contrary.

In the case of manic behavior, which might be described as frantic behavior, there is a recurring pattern of rapid flight of ideas, speech, or action accompanied by sleeplessness, extreme excitement or agitation. Manic behavior could take the form of grandiosity, buying or planning sprees, or even sexual indiscretions, and the person has no awareness of the consequences.

Manic behavior is not to be confused with the normal high energy that some people exhibit in their attempt to accomplish their goals in the world, find a mate, or realize a career. For highly motivated people, it is natural for large amounts of energy to be directed out into the world to accomplish their dreams. In their enthusiasm, high energy people have not lost touch with everyday reality.

At the opposite end of the spectrum of psychotic behavior called manic is a prolonged, disoriented, morbid, or withdrawn vegetative depression with no insight or desire for relief. Often there is a swing between these two extremes in the same person, referred to as manic-depressive.

A referral to a mental health professional or facility needs to be made if psychosis is suspected or presented. Medication is usually prescribed.

Depression—There is also another more prevalent kind of depression which is not psychotic in nature. Today in America, more than 2.5 million people suffer from this depression and it occurs at any age, with either sex, regardless of family circumstances, status, or career. Again, referral to a mental health professional is in order.

Because depression is so prevalent, people need to know some of the symptoms. These include diminished interest or pleasure in all, or almost all, activities most of the day, nearly every day; significant weight loss or weight gain; insomnia or excessive sleeping nearly every day; fatigue or loss of energy nearly every day; feelings of worthlessness or guilt nearly every day; indecisiveness or diminished ability to think or concentrate; thoughts of death, along with ideas about suicide. A specific plan for suicide may or may not exist, but an attempt at committing suicide could occur.

Depression has been a factor in a number of illustrative cases already presented. Being "on your own" goes a long way toward overcoming depression. Counseling or therapy is also recommended for those who get stuck.

A Word of Caution and Some Helpful Guidelines

Care must be taken not to identify every mental disturbance people exhibit as psychotic or serious, especially those behaviors that disturb observers more than those suffering some of the symptoms. Following is a simple criterion to determine the difference:

Length of the Disturbance—Mental disturbances may appear sporadically during erratic growth of older adolescents into adulthood or periodically at any time during someone's life. These symptoms will persist only for brief periods of time—no more than a few days. During this time, friends and relatives help most by using their best listening skills and trying to assist the person to help himself, usually with coping in an extremely stressful situation.

Consistency of the Disturbance—The appearance and disappearance, or the waxing and waning, of mental disturbances can be signs of growth or manageable stress release. When the symptoms are constant and extend over long periods of time, they are indicative of more serious psychological problems.

Consequences of the Disturbance—The results of the disturbances are harmless, benign, and not physically dangerous to the person or to others. If this is the case, it is more likely the disturbance reflects a natural process of throwing off excessive stress or a person's lack of more appropriate coping skills. It is not usually a sign of mental illness.

Awareness of the Disturbance—The person can reflect upon himself by talking about the disturbance, admitting its inappropriateness, understanding its possible source and course, seeing it as a by-product of some particular strains or stress in life, and agreeing to take some action to help stabilize the situation. Awareness of the disturbance is the most important indication that the person has the capacity ultimately to understand and deal with his own problem.

Self-referrals and referrals by others to licensed health practitioners, such as psychologists and psychiatrists, increases the likelihood that services rendered will be within the professional's expertise. They know when and to whom to make other appropriate referrals if the problem is outside their area of competence.

Suicide—Finally, what does one do if someone very dear or very close threatens to or actually commits suicide? As a rule, thoughts or talk about suicide are not sufficient to determine serious suicide risk conclusively. However, when expressions about suicide are accompanied by one or more of the following criteria, the risk factor for suicide increases progressively.

1. A person openly expresses clear intent to commit suicide.
2. Concrete plans for suicide are devised and discussed.
3. Lethal means such as guns or hanging are considered, or the person acquires unusual, potentially dangerous items.

4. A history of previous suicide attempts exists.
5. Person engages in termination behavior, such as writing a suicide note or giving favorite things away.
6. Person exhibits impulsive behavior, such as quitting a job, running away, overdosing drugs or alcohol, displaying inappropriate and intense anger or rage, or takes sudden and unreasonable risks. These abrupt changes in behavior contrast to previous patterns.
7. A history of drug and alcohol abuse exists.
8. Person lacks a support system or supportive people in his or her life.
9. A recent crisis was experienced, such as the death of a loved one, separation, divorce, arrest, loss of job, income, or home.
10. There is a history of depression in the person's life, or the recent sudden lifting of a depression.

Again, we emphasize that contact with and referral to a licensed mental health professional or suicide prevention agency are necessary. This time, however, the referral needs to be immediate.

The referral agency will advise whether it is also necessary to notify other family members, college personnel, employers, or friends. At this point, a qualified professional needs to be direct and talk openly with the person about suicide. This is not the time to argue, lecture, or moralize. Nor is it the time to panic or over-react. It is the time to seek professional guidance, even if the person refuses.

The following case history was one of the more painful we encountered in our many years of counseling and therapy. It was also the acid test of the principles in this book, **On Your Own.**

Tim and Sara were a respected middle aged couple actively involved in helping others professionally and in many community, volunteer projects. Both had come from families where the parents continued to have a strong influence on decisions, support, and directions in their lives. They both were strongly committed to helping their children with as much education as the children desired and were quite accepting of a prolonged period of relative financial dependency on the part of their children.

Their son, Michael, one of three grown children, had recently graduated from college, but was having difficulty deciding on a career track. Michael had established contact with a self-improvement group that his parents knew little about but advertised itself as helping people develop themselves and their job skills to the fullest in order to achieve success in life.

Suddenly one morning Michael announced to his mother that he was moving to the city where the self-improvement center was located. Once separated from his parents, Michael strove to be independent. He did not ask his parents for financial help even though the job he had expected at the self-improvement center turned out to be a dead-end. Michael finally found a job as a day laborer—the only non-minority member of his work group. After an argument with the foreman, Michael was not asked to return.

Michael's parents had not seen him for some time, and they were becoming increasingly concerned. Tim and Sara tried to reestablish communication and encouraged him to come home. Michael subsequently did return agitated and enraged, and Sara, sensing Michael's rage and bitter disappointment, tried to persuade him to go with her to see a local counselor. To no avail. Michael refused and stormed back to the city. Since Tim and Sara were unable to make further contact with Michael, that was the last time they saw their son alive.

As is often the case with suicides, no one suspected how deeply depressed Michael had become. Michael's desire to individuate from his parents and to establish his independence both financially and ego/emotionally left him particularly vulnerable at this time in his life. Michael had transferred his dependency on his parents to dependency on a self-help organization which made ever increasing financial demands on him.

Neither his parents, from whom Michael had separated himself, nor the movement which had ignorantly and irresponsibly dropped him when his anger surfaced, realized the intensity and the depth of depression Michael was experiencing. Furthermore, because of the organization's opposition to psychiatry and psychology, Michael never got the reputable, professional help that might have steered him away from his final decision.

When Michael's parents came for therapy, they needed to move through the normal, natural process of grief. This included working through the denial, anger, and depression. The process was important, but just as important was the need for them to work through their abnormal and unnatural guilt.

In retrospect, Tim and Sara were able to understand the array of circumstances that led to Michael's suicide: his vocational plight; his association with a dangerous cult; some abuse of alcohol and drugs during his college years; a history of impulsive behavior; and a nagging lack of self-esteem related to a learning disability. But Tim and Sara initially felt most of these symptoms resulted because they were bad parents. They felt they had failed to rescue their son.

As the months passed, the normal, natural grieving began to lift. In therapy they were able to see that they were not letting go of their son—they were still parenting. They also began to see that their guilt was based on their own self-condemnation and low self-esteem. The constant blaming of themselves was a habit they had acquired when they were younger. Because of this habit of blaming themselves, they were unable to accept and feel good about themselves. Emotionally and egoically, their growth had been arrested. In a very real sense, most of their lives had been spent in the roles of children or parents. It was time for them to be on their own—as adults.

When they began to accept themselves, they were able finally to accept the behavior of their dead son and process the anger they felt for a son who had taken himself away from them forever. It was not until Tim and Sara were able to let go of their own fears of not having been good enough, that they could accept (a) they had done the best that they could while their son was alive; (b) they thought it was OK at the time; and, (c) the fact that it did not work out didn't change this. They needed to understand with their entire being that they chose only their actions, NOT the outcome. Finally, they were able to let go of their guilt.

No one can live someone else's life for them, even when that someone is as close as a son or daughter or spouse or elderly parent. We were reassured to know that the principles in this book helped this couple to not only relieve their pain, but also to release the fear of not being good enough that inevitably underlies guilt.

We want to alert readers to another situation that can arise involving the threat of suicide. The situation occurs when someone uses the threat of suicide to manipulate another person into doing what the threatener wants. Because people being threatened fear that someone they care about will actually commit suicide, they continue to reinforce the threats by giving in to them. At some point, this manipulative behavior must stop for both parties to be able to disengage from the pattern and become independent.

An example that clearly illustrates the kind of manipulative behavior that can take the form of threats of suicide occurred between a single middle aged parent named Debra and her 25 year-old son, Grant. Debra, a widow, was left in very comfortable economic circumstances and she held an influential position in society. Because of her circumstances she was able to use her many connections, both business and social, to help her son attend the best colleges and obtain jobs. Unfortunately, her son failed out and dropped out of two of the colleges, and he either quit the jobs his mother helped him get or was fired.

Each time Grant failed at another opportunity his mother had helped him obtain, he returned to live at home mildly depressed or arrogantly defiant. He quickly slipped into a pattern of staying out late at night, coming home drunk, sleeping late, and refusing to work or help in any way around the house. If his mother insisted that he try to find work or that he go back to school or that he stop drinking and staying out late every night, he would threaten her with suicide. Inevitably, Debra would retreat from her position and quietly permit Grant to continue his irresponsible behavior.

Debra feared the loss of her son. She also feared social rejection and was very concerned that others would think she was a bad mother, especially if Grant were to follow through on his suicide threats. Grant refused to go for therapy of any kind and ridiculed his mother's concern with such statements as, "You'd be happy if I were dead." "You never cared about me, only about what other people think." And so it went on.

Debra recounted to us the final incident that proved to be the key in turning the dilemma around. One night after Grant returned home following a night of drinking, she told him that he would have to get a job, move out, and be on his own, that she would not tolerate his threats or support his life style any longer. Grant grabbed a butcher knife and lay down on the kitchen floor with the knife ready to pierce his throat. Debra didn't know what possessed her at the time, but to her own amazement, she stood over him and told Grant in no uncertain terms that she was not responsible for his life and if he wanted to commit suicide that was his decision and she could not stop him. Grant knew that his mother meant every word she said. He put the butcher knife down, got up, and from that moment began the slow, but steady, progress toward recovery.

While this is a dramatic example of someone using the threat of suicide to avoid being independent and to manipulate another person, it makes the point. We don't advise handling suicide threats on this "showdown" basis, but we need to keep in mind that all suicide threats do not result in death. It is best to consult with a professional when suicide threats are present.

We have tried to provide you with a fairly complete, but by no means exhaustive list of mental health problems which would require referral and special consideration. Primarily our suggestions have reiterated the need to seek help from health or helping professionals and the information needed about the behaviors and symptoms that signal serious concern.

There are other concerns which may be considered more social in nature but also have a mental health component. These are actions taken by a person that do not support his or her life, the lives for whom they bear some responsibility, or the life of the community as a whole. Some examples of what we mean are:

squander or gamble money that would deprive an
individual or his family of basic necessities;

withdraw from society to the extent that the individual is unable to function socially in the most
fundamental ways;

present a personal physical appearance or living
circumstance that is not only offensive, but also
unhealthy or illegal;

abandon family and family responsibilities;

violate the rights of others or become physically
abusive;

commit criminal offenses.

In some cases, the family of the individual might be able to rectify the problem. If they cannot, then referral should be made to the appropriate individual or agency which might include marriage, family, financial, or employment counselors; social workers, welfare agencies, rehabilitation counselors; drug and alcohol centers, family service centers or hospitals. In some cases (such as abuse and criminal behavior), it may be necessary or even legally required to contact the police, domestic, or child abuse centers.

The best referral is self-referral, but we have also seen that referral by another may also be necessary in certain cases. Obviously, other circumstances could arise where good judgement would need to be exercised. Finally, if in doubt, the best motto is "safety first." We are confident that all of the mental health difficulties that people experience can be significantly helped by being "on their own."

Disabling Physical Illness

A disabling or terminal illness ranks high on the list of life's stressful events. When it strikes people tend to think of the person as being necessarily debilitated and frequently use such terms as "total disability" or "unable to care for oneself." Those in the helping professions are quick to point out, however, that even when working with a disabled or terminally ill person, "pity" has no place because pity reinforces the illness. What needs to be reinforced are the person's strengths as the adult they are.

What follows are two remarkable examples of how a renewed sense of independence helped a very disabled and terminally ill woman and an elderly but capable gentleman live out their final years with adult-like dignity. Each rose to the challenge of their circumstances and was able to serve as an inspiration to others.

Veronica, a 36 year-old woman, was diagnosed as being "totally disabled" with multiple sclerosis which required full-time nursing home care. During her recent and first nursing home confinement, she went into a depression, prayed for death, and refused to leave her room to eat or to be seen by other residents. She was also troubled and shamed by her problem with incontinence. Initially, she had refused counseling, but had finally agreed to one session.

During that counseling session, we learned that Veronica had embarked upon a much desired social work career at the age of 22. It was at that time when the first symptoms of multiple sclerosis appeared. She had always been a self-reliant, outspoken person who took pride in helping others.

In fact, part of Veronica's frustration at being in a nursing home was "seeing all the suffering and not being able to help." She had resented the gradual deterioration of her physical condition over the years so much that she frequently insisted on doing such things as washing and dressing herself even after she was largely incapable of doing so. Now in the nursing home and depressed, Veronica became uncooperative, ashamed, and acted helpless even in the areas where she could still perform, such as going to the dining room or conversing with other residents, or even pushing the buzzer when she had to urinate.

Good counseling rapport was established with Veronica and a number of her "shoulds," "oughts," and "musts" regarding her condition were refuted for more rational thinking. She began to accept where she was, and what was happening to her. Eventually she came to realize that the finest way she could help others in the nursing home was to be an inspiration to them. Because Veronica was younger than the other nursing home residents and because her disability was more tragic, other residents cared about her.

Veronica agreed to start eating in the dining room. Her cheerfulness, although forced at first, quickly received positive responses from others, and she knew it and liked it. Next she agreed to visit daily with another patient who had a disabling illness. These talks helped Veronica as much as the other resident.

A behavior modification program for incontinence was initiated, and Veronica agreed to cooperate, which resulted in some improvement. She also began spending 2-3 hours daily watching and listening to audio and video tapes. Once again she took up reading for enrichment. Gradually, her depression lifted and Veronica was able to spend her remaining days being the inspirational social worker she had always wanted to be.

This case is a dramatic example of how being "on your own," in whatever capacity one can, is vital to growth no matter what stage in life or what circumstances prevail. Since growth is a primary fact of life, it can even overshadow illness and impending death.

John, 77 years-old, was referred to us by his life-time friend and physician after he became a resident in a local nursing home. John's psychological symptoms were major depression with suicidal tendencies. When first seen in the nursing home exhibiting classic symptoms of depression and withdrawal, it was hard to believe that only a short time ago this man was a robust senior citizen.

Although his physical problems were not major, the medical staff expected him to be a permanent resident of the nursing home for the rest of his life. They had seen many other cases like John's. But John's case ended up defying all expectations.

John's depressed condition was brought on by the death of his spouse of 50 years, whom he dearly loved. They lived in the same apartment for more than 40 years, never had any children, and despite his wife's physical difficulties related to arthritis, they cared for each other quite well. They enjoyed their time together and were active in the community.

John's 76 year-old wife died under tragic circumstances which left him burdened with guilt and hopelessness. He and his wife were about to leave for a week-end vacation, something they enjoyed doing together quite frequently. While backing the car out of the driveway he bumped his wife who was standing nearby and couldn't move quickly enough to step aside. Complications developed related to her broken hip, and she died several weeks later.

The death of a spouse is one of life's most stressful events under the most ordinary circumstances. In John's case the event was coupled with his overwhelming sense of responsibility for having caused her death. What John experienced as a result of his wife's death is what could be called a regression phenomena. John had lived a normal life of adult responsibility and was a stable, healthy adult. This crisis disoriented John so much that he reverted to the immature defense mechanism of withdrawal from life.

John blamed himself for her death and believed he deserved to die also. A tranquilizing drug and a major antidepressant were prescribed because of his threatening mental condition. When we started working with John, he revealed that he never wanted to return to his apartment, nor did he even want to return to life itself. Ordinarily under these circumstances, a man his age would have spent the rest of his life in the nursing home.

But John had inadvertently revealed that since his wife's death, he did not really believe that he could live alone because he never had done so in his entire life. Typical of so many men of his era, John didn't even know how to boil water, let alone how to keep house. In this aspect of life, John was as apprehensive as any adolescent afraid to move out on his own for the first time.

The most important task in counseling with John was to help him overcome his guilt over the circumstances of his wife's death. He began to let go of telling himself he "should have seen her," and accepted that what had happened was not his fault. Slowly he worked through his grief. But in the process of working through this obstacle, it became more and more apparent that John's lack of self-confidence and fear of not being able to take care of himself was the barrier separating John from returning to a normal life.

Finally John agreed to participate in an experiment. We arranged for him to go home to his apartment on a week-end pass. If it didn't work out, he could return at any time. Fortunately his pension adequately supported him, and he certainly was familiar with his surroundings. Arrangements had been made for a social worker to assist John with shopping and with some basic meal planning and preparation skills. A neighbor was alerted to visit him. We had agreed to be on call.

John's week-end pass was successful, but not without difficulties. Everything from learning how to light a stove to running a vacuum cleaner was new to John. But after a few week-end passes, John said he was ready to try a week-long pass. By this time, John was less dependent on the drugs he had been taking and his depression significantly improved.

John's counseling continued at home. He regularly visited his physician for his minor aches and pains, but soon no
longer needed to take tranquilizers or anti-depressants. He
learned to participate in the senior citizen activities that were
available and started to venture out more and more.

What had happened to John because of this crisis was a
text book example of the growth of independence to the fullest
extent possible in this man's life. Physically he was taking care
of himself in ways he had never done before in his life.
Socially, he could now avail himself of support systems that
enriched his life. John had already been well developed on the
ego/emotional, moral, and intellectual level, which enabled
him to overcome his guilt over the circumstances of his wife's
death. His financial independence was the result of a life-time
of confidently providing for himself and his wife. The conditions which caused John to regress to dependent behavior had
been overcome through John's own commitment to live the full
life of an adult as much as possible again.

Crisis at Retirement

It is interesting that retirement is also high on the list of
life's most stressful events. One would think that a retirement
which was long anticipated would not only be a relief, but the
beginning of happy stress-free times. For many this simply is
not so—particularly for those who find themselves with much
idle time on their hands and no sense of achievement or
purpose. All of this can mean the onset of dependency accompanied by depression.

An example which will help illustrate our point is 65 year-
old Leonard, who had always been a high achiever and a very
busy man. His job as a construction supervisor required long
hours and meticulous attention to details, time-tables, and
organization, all of which suited his compulsive nature well.
Compulsory (an enigma to a compulsive!) retirement came in
November and with it Leonard and his wife left their Pennsylvania home for the first time in January, along with the other
"snowbirds" heading for Florida.

It took all of three weeks for Leonard, not a sun worshipper, to get bored with the routine. He did nothing and had no sense of achievement. He started worrying about his carefully tended home in Pennsylvania, wondering whether the furnace was working or the pipes were frozen, whether the automatic lights were effectively thwarting burglars. A latent obsessive-compulsive tendency rose to the surface regarding his home. Since he was helpless to do anything about the house from 1500 miles away, he felt hopeless and became depressed.

Reduced in Florida to lying on the couch worrying all day, not eating much or sleeping at night, and with his sex life deteriorated, Leonard returned a wreck to Pennsylvania in March. When we saw him, he was shaky, barely functioning, and on a high dose of tranquilizers. He had also become very dependent on his concerned wife for the smallest things.

Most professionals in the field of psychology know that obsessive compulsive tendencies are resistant to therapy—particularly in the elderly. Leonard was not about to change his habits or his basic personality at age 65! So the question was what to do with Leonard. "Something to do" seemed to hold promise in Leonard's case, since having nothing to do appeared to have precipitated his disorder and dependency.

During the course of some painfully slow progress in therapy it was discovered that Leonard, an ex-Navy man, liked boats. Not only did he like boating, he liked working mechanically on boats. Unfortunately, he didn't own a boat because he never had the time for one while he was employed. Also, since Leonard was basically a tightwad and feared any financial loss, he would never have bought a boat even though he could have afforded one.

Through much encouragement and confrontation in therapy, and with the ultimatum "buy one or else" from his now angry wife, Leonard relented and purchased a rather expensive boat. During that first summer following the return from Florida, Leonard played with his new boat and learned everything he could about it. He went at this task much the same as he did most things—compulsively.

Soon Leonard's depression lifted and he discontinued his medication. Come January he faced his fears and returned to Florida. There he not only spent much time with his boat, but also spent his remaining time fixing the boats of neighbors and friends, earning a little "under the table" income for his efforts.

Leonard was once again a very busy and happy man. He still thought about his empty house in Pennsylvania, but he could put the thoughts aside when he asked and answered for himself, "What's the worst thing that could happen, and is that so bad?"

Leonard had been well on his way to becoming a depressed, helpless, and drug-dependent person. The key in his case was taking the big first step by buying the boat and returning to Florida. He acted rather than reacted, did it for himself, and was "on his own.".

Many of the cases in this chapter were taken from experiences in counseling and therapy. When difficult situations arise and neither the person nor family or friends are successful in alleviating the problems, we have recommended seeking outside assistance. We are by no means implying that everyone must go for help in order to finally be on one's own. We also acknowledge that it is possible, in some cases, for people to become dependent on the services of helping professionals or other resources and thus defeat the goal of becoming independent. We are aware, as perhaps are many of our readers, of numerous cases where people have individuated, even under the most difficult of circumstances, without the necessity for outside assistance. We hope this book will increase that number.

Chapter Six
Adulthood and the Expansion of Awareness

Chapter Six briefly explains why it is necessary to become an individuated adult before a person can more fully expand awareness and become established in higher states of consciousness. This section is of particular interest to anyone who has been involved in or is considering involvement in personal growth groups or consciousness expansion movements or who is practicing techniques or following a teacher or a unique life-style aimed at self-improvement. It confronts the tacit assumption shared by many, if not most, of those involved in such efforts, that independent adulthood has already been achieved. Such is not usually the case. It demonstrates how there can be no sustained transcending as long as a person is defending an arrested, regressed, and dependent ego/emotional character structure. Unnecessary dependence on teachers, programs, and movements is also discussed.

In order to make the link or bridge between adult independence and what is called expanded awareness, we need to recall the six major areas of development discussed earlier. You will remember that we said the area of ego/emotional development was the most difficult one in which to establish independence. That's because the feelings or emotions that are experienced and the ego or the concept people have about themselves are both the subtlest and deepest aspect of the personality and the most powerful as well.

If people look at personality as the sum total of all that makes them the individuals they are, then it includes the following full range of characteristics, from the grossest to the subtlest. These include the physical body and senses, the meanings or perceptions that attach to whatever is sensed, the intellect which reasons and discriminates, the emotions or feelings that are experienced, and the ego or self-concept which is thoughts people have about themselves. These personality attributes correspond roughly to the six major areas of development discussed earlier.

We have chosen to consider the ego and emotions together as the most influential aspect of the personality because they are the most subtle and powerful. It is not uncommon for people, for example, to experience how feelings such as fear, anger, and guilt can override both intellect and common sense, and cause them to behave irrationally. At the same time, a self-concept such as, "I am not good enough; I should be better than I am," can influence behavior and feelings dramatically.

In advocating ego/emotional independence, we have seen the necessity to work through fears, anger, and guilt, along with the negative, limited concepts people may have had about themselves. In the process they become aware of how they blame or assign responsibility for how they feel, and particularly how they feel about themselves, to other people, situations, and things. When they are able to refute irrational "shoulds," "oughts," and "musts" they have discovered how to go beyond an ego-emotionally dependent posture.

Put more concretely, they spontaneously replace, within their lives and vocabularies, the dependent phrase, "You make me feel so bad" with "I am responsible for what I feel by virtue of what I tell myself." Likewise, "I am not good enough; I should be better than I am because others think so or they say so," becomes "I am who I am and that's all who I am right now, and I'm OK no matter what anybody says or thinks."

In this manner, they separate themselves from underdeveloped, arrested, or regressed child-adolescent dependencies, and they become developed, released, established, independent adults. Once this is accomplished, what comes next? Is that all there is?

At this point, each of us can ask ourselves a series of probing questions. Is the development of the ego, the subtlest and most powerful aspect of our personality, and the establishment of its independence, the final outcome of growth? Since the ego, or self-concept is the nucleus of concepts or thoughts we have about ourselves and who we are, is that what and who we are? Are we just a collection of thoughts? Who is it that is thinking these thoughts anyway? If the ego is a collection of thoughts, how can it be the thinker of thoughts too? Where do thoughts come from anyway? Who is the "I" that is thinking? Is there somebody or something beyond thought?

When we reach the point of this maddening and circuitous questioning, the time has come to go beyond the ego—beyond a limited "conception" of who we are, to a boundless "experience" of who we are. That experience is what can be called awareness—awareness itself—awareness beyond thought. It is not that the ego becomes more aware, since the ego is just a collection of thoughts incapable of being aware in and of itself. Rather as awareness expands, there is less identification with the ego and more realization of one's essential nature as awareness itself.

Awareness itself is the foundation of all thoughts. Awareness is the basis of thought itself in the sense that thoughts are the manifestation or vibration of awareness. Imagine that awareness is like a backdrop of a stage. Upon that stage there are different actors playing different roles in life, but the backdrop always remains the same. Or think of awareness itself as a movie screen. Different images are continually flashing on it, but the screen itself never changes. Without the stage or the screen, there can be no actors acting or images flashing. Awareness is the most profound basis, the basis that is always there throughout all of the different roles, feelings, thoughts, and activities. Awareness is us.

The establishment of awareness as an all-time conscious reality is enlightenment or the wisdom that "I am awareness itself" which grows to encompass "we are awareness itself." The realization that "all this is awareness itself" is the culmination of wisdom. The "concept" of awareness itself as us once seemed very abstract and philosophical. But today many people are beginning to "experience" expanded awareness itself as a living reality, and that experience has a profound effect in their daily lives.

It is here that each one makes the link between expanded awareness and adult independence. In order to expand awareness, it is necessary to go beyond child-adolescent dependence to adult independence. To be adult is to be established in ego/emotional independence—free from the need to defend an underdeveloped, arrested, regressed, or weakened ego/emotional structure. For as long as a person identifies with and is defending a weakened ego/emotional structure, he or she can not transcend or go beyond it on a sustained basis. Thus adult independence becomes the link or bridge to more fully expanded awareness.

An example of a case can help illustrate what we mean. Angelica, 38 years-old and single, came for therapy, depressed and down on herself. The man with whom she had been in a serious relationship had left her. She remembered having felt the same way some fifteen years previously when another man had broken off a relationship with her. At the same time she was blaming these men for the way she felt, she was also blaming herself.

Angelica's mother and sister both received their share of blame from Angelica for the anger and hurt she was experiencing. To add further to the difficulties, Angelica's diminished self-esteem and lack of confidence caused her to stay at home crying, rather then face her job as a sales representative. Thus she was having financial problems, too.

During discussions, Angelica revealed that although she was now frustrated and felt "stuck," at one time she had been a seeker, and to some extent, a "finder" of meaning and wholeness in her life. A philosophy graduate, she had read many books on life, spirituality, and consciousness. A regular practitioner of meditation and visualization techniques, Angelica had numerous experiences of what she called "bliss" and "oneness with nature."

Angelica was able not only to astutely analyze her dreams after she had them, but also to change them while she was dreaming. She experienced being a "witness" to her dreams. Many of these dreams had come true for her, as did many of her intuitions about others and the future. She felt she could communicate with animals and young pre-verbal children. All these experiences, however, had now stopped, and she found herself blocked, hopeless, and doubting the validity of the very experiences she had treasured. In her words, she stated, "I feel I am off my path."

In therapeutically tracing back the fear and loneliness she was feeling, a small and wounded child within was discovered. When Angelica was seven years old, the family moved from one state to another. Uprooted from familiar, small town living to a strange place, people and circumstances, she remembered with pain how she cried for days with her head down on her desk in her new classroom. She also remembered her mother's fear, discontent, and refusal to get involved in the new community. Here is where Angelica's ego/emotional development was arrested and her dependency continued.

Somewhat astonished when confronted with having to back up and grow up, Angelica courageously accepted and continued therapy. Irrational assumptions and blaming with regard to how others "should" treat her were refuted. An affirmation technique to bolster her self-image by changing her negative thoughts about herself was practiced. She made herself face her fears and tears, and she went back out to work. Her depression lifted, her confidence returned, and her financial condition improved.

What was more telling, however, was that all the experiences and signs of expanded awareness returned. Angelica had backed up and grown up egoically and emotionally in order to continue "on her path." In this sense, then, adult independence is seen as the basis for the growth of awareness and adult independence is what this book is all about.

When all of us pause and wonder what the twenty-first century will be like, we get excited, curious, maybe even apprehensive. Many envision the coming of a new age when collective human awareness will have expanded much closer to its full potential. They see humanity overcoming ominous problems that have plagued the world, even as we write these words, such as war, economic collapse, and environmental disasters. They predict that people will live in higher states of awareness. But is this just another utopian pipe dream preceding the turn of yet another century?

In contrast to sceptics and those who foresee doom for humanity are individuals in increasing numbers, like Angelica, who claim direct experiences of life from an expanded and holistic perspective. Representing every strata of society, they make it harder to dismiss their experiences about intimately perceiving all life as part of themselves. They give renewed meaning to the idea of oneness.

On Your Own has not focused on specific techniques to attain expanded awareness, nor does it deal with the psychological disturbances accompanying the growth of awareness. **On Your Own** emphasizes complete understanding and experience of the process of becoming adult, a relative process that must unfold individually before someone can permanently establish higher states of awareness. Psychological disturbances accompanying the growth of awareness are dealt with in an earlier book co-authored by us called **Growing Sane** (Upshur Press, 1991).

Growing Sane more fully defines awareness (or consciousness as it is called in that book) and systematically addresses problems that people encounter once they have begun to experience expanded states of consciousness. It does not matter what techniques they may have used or to what movement or programs they belong.

Whether people follow established programs for personal growth or develop in their own way, understanding growth "per se" broadens the ability to comprehend what exactly is happening to them. Growth is natural and eventually occurs despite what people tell themselves along the way, and no matter how many obstacles they must overcome. Understanding makes the process easier and helps stabilize the gains. We emphasize that growth does not stop once people become adults. Evolution is a fact of life.

For many individuals, growth may mean having to "back up" and "grow up" in areas or stages of life that were missed, glossed over, or put aside as unworthy of attention. Far too many "seekers" after truth are stuck at the child-adolescent or parental stages, neither having established adulthood nor experienced being "on their own." Their experiences of expanded awareness do indeed expose the fear, anger, and guilt associated with dependency but they do little or nothing to actually address what has been exposed. They mistakenly believe they can substitute experiences of expanded awareness for the prerequisite of "growing up." In making this mistake, they accomplish neither goal.

Our experience in the practice of counseling and therapy confirms that many, if not most, individuals "along the path" to higher consciousness have to back up and do some work in order to become independent adults. Perhaps they have never held a steady job or earned enough money to provide for their own needs. Many have not adjusted to society outside of their own growth or spiritual group, but rather they remain child-adolescents in their interpersonal relationships.

Most growth of consciousness groups or spiritual movements assume that the people who come to them are already adults; thus, they offer little help to those who are not. This is particularly so in western culture where the tradition has been on independence and individuality. There is a tendency to disparage as unnecessary or even damaging those techniques or methods which can facilitate adult independence. Frequently the rationale for "unnecessary" is based upon the belief that the groups or movements have all that it takes to fulfill a person's needs. They contend that other techniques are damaging because they focus attention unduly on the "negative" or problem aspects of life, and this emphasis on negativity is non-life supporting.

Our response to that position is to question the basic assumption that "seekers" necessarily are adults simply because they seek a higher level of truth. Our experience confirms that this simply and frequently is just not so. Most movements that can sustain themselves over any length of time are discovering this as well. Ultimately, meditation and other related techniques result in transcendence of the ego, emotions, and even problems of life. That is not to say that from time to time we can't have transcendent experiences. We can settle down and occasionally slip past those distractions. However, the permanence or stabilization of the transcendent experience will remain elusive. Also, we transcend the ego more easily when it is strong and individuated, rather than weak.

As we said, if your ego/emotional nature is weak, you will unconsciously defend yourself through blame, attack, misplaced anger, avoidance, repression, rationalization, or any of the other defense mechanisms. **As long as there is defending, there can be no complete transcending. This is so because when we are defending our egos, we are not letting go. And letting go is necessary for transcending.** Transcendence of ego identification is necessary for enlightenment. While it is so that eastern cultures by virtue of their conditioning emphasize submission and surrender of the ego, it is also so that western cultural conditioning emphasizes the strengthening and individuation of the ego. Both are viable paths.

Imagine what would happen if someone in a weakened physical state because of hunger approached a master teacher for guidance. Most likely, the teacher would bring the seeker in and give him something to eat first. Similarly, we strongly urge seekers who need to back up and grow up to do so now. Sharpen your interpersonal skills and face your fears of abandonment or rejection in all areas of life. This is essential.

If you can't improve your interpersonal skills on your own, get help from a counselor or therapist who is experienced in working with personality disorders and interpersonal breakdowns. If the counselor or therapist knows about the growth of consciousness, then so much the better. If not, go ahead anyway. Use this book as a manual for understanding the growth of consciousness, and fill in the spaces yourself. Eventually it has to be done anyway!

Occasionally people have asked if becoming an independent adult is tantamount to becoming enlightened. We appreciate the question because it emphasizes the need to clarify carefully the subtle distinctions between the two. Becoming an independent adult means we are comfortably and solidly established in our bodies, senses, perceptions, intellects, emotions, and egos–or at least well on the way to that end.

Being enlightened means we have transcended our bodies, senses, perceptions, intellects, emotions, and egos both in and out of normal daily activity because we are established permanently in Being. Therefore, we need to become an adult before we can be enlightened. We can ultimately transcend the qualities of adulthood, but we can not by-pass these qualities.

While it is true that becoming fully adult is an immediate stepping stone to enlightenment, the two states will probably overlap from time to time along the way. But since the steps of progress can be two steps forward and one step back, the step backward may be necessary, especially when we need to back up and grow up before we can continue.

Growing Sane, pp. 61-63

Because more and more people are reporting deeper and broader experiences of that one reality called consciousness or awareness, the need is even greater for recognition and understanding, along with measures and techniques to stabilize, integrate, and encourage the smooth continuation of this process. Globally, the dramatic effects of more people "growing sane" through continued expansion of science and technology, responsible environmental action, the social, political, and economic unity of nations, and the prospects for world peace are evident. Even with the inevitable setbacks, the overall effect still has been encouraging.

The primary necessity for those "on the path" to enlightenment is to become adults through successfully accomplishing what readers of **On Your Own** have come to understand as "separation-individuation." Adult independence needs to occur physically, intellectually, socially, morally, financial/vocationally, and ego/emotionally.

The effect of expanded awareness on society and future generations produces a wealth of inspiring speculation. But recognition of the prerequisite for growing up is humbling as well as necessary for those in search of "higher" truth, more profound meaning in their own lives, and the dawning of a new age. There are, however, potential problems of becoming unnecessarily <u>dependent</u> on teachers, programs, or movements as the following example illustrates.

When Thomas was 20 years-old and in college, he became an ardent member and practitioner of a Christian religion . He read extensively, prayed, went to church regularly, and participated in all the rites and rituals, scrupulously trying to avoid sin and obey the rules and regulations of his religion. From time to time, he experienced satisfaction, inner peace, and spiritual wholeness. However, just as often, he found himself bound up and feeling guilty because he had not lived up to those rules and regulations. He questioned many of them, but he quickly put the questions aside and took the rules and regulations on "faith."

Thomas continued living in this way, but not without recognizing his increasing frustration, anxiety, obsessions with sin, and compulsive rituals to cleanse himself of such sins. Thomas had learned, and it seemed he had been taught, among other things, that sex was sinful. What ensued was a painful struggle resulting in much sex repression. But all of this was, as he saw it, adherence to the teachings of his religion, and he would stick with it.

Marriage for Thomas seemed to put many of his sexual problems on the back burner. However, a new problem developed. He was unable to convince his wife that his religion was the best one. She thought other Christian religions were just as good. The showdown came one Sunday when she refused to go to his church because it was uninspiring and she wanted to go elsewhere. Previously he had brow-beaten her into attending his church because it was mandatory for him. Faced with having to choose between his religion and his wife, he took a big risk, made the leap, chose his wife, and went to church elsewhere.

It was a turning point in his life. His new-found freedom allowed him to think, act, and feel in ways he had never done before. He sought therapy for the obsessions and compulsions he had developed because of the sexual repression and he made significant progress. Oddly enough, his understanding and experience of Christianity broadened and deepened, so much so that he began to embrace the world's other religions as well. This is how it went for several years... quite well.

As Thomas' enchantment with spirituality increased, so did his understanding of other fundamental teachings. Wanting to supplement that understanding with his own direct experience, he convinced himself that he needed a wise teacher who would show him how to obtain those experiences for himself. Thomas found a teacher from the east who taught him techniques to expand consciousness.

Through conscientious practice, Thomas experienced, in a way that he had never done before, what he referred to as inner clarity, peace, and wholeness. He joined the movement associated with the teacher, and once again became an ardent member and practitioner. He read extensively, meditated, went to meetings, participated in all the rites and rituals, and scrupulously tried to obey all the rules and regulations. Once again, Thomas felt bound up, anxious, and guilty.

Older and wiser, a middle aged Thomas began to see the root of the problem himself. While deeply appreciative of what the teacher had imparted, Thomas disassociated himself from the movement and even let go of his attachment for the teacher as his only source of guidance. He recognized, as is often the case, that it wasn't the teacher he had difficulty with as much as it was the movement which supposedly represented the teacher. Movements frequently have a way of getting out of hand, misinterpreting, and misrepresenting a particular teaching without the teacher even knowing.

It was another turning point in Thomas' life. This time his new-found freedom allowed him to trust his own intuition more. As time went by, Thomas felt the "teacher within" guiding him toward rewarding experiences he had never had before. If he got stuck, he turned to respected teachers in print or in person, but then moved on quickly. He dropped his unnecessary dependency on teachers, programs, and movements. Thomas had grown up.

We are sharply aware that in suggesting independence from teachers, programs, or movements, we are on delicate ground. If people are to become independent of such teachers, programs, or movements, does it not also mean that they should become independent of such organizations as alcohol and drug support groups? How long does someone need to be dependent upon support groups? Is recovery from any and all dependency difficulties a lifetime program of "recovery" in which there can never be anyone who is "recovered?"

In order to answer these seemingly puzzling questions, it is necessary to remember that growth itself is a lifetime program and that it proceeds from stage to stage. Keeping this in mind, one can see that just as a person proceeds from crawling to walking and from childhood to adolescence, it is also possible to proceed from adolescence to adulthood. While recognizing the necessity for some people who have permanent disabilities to remain in a particular program for a lifetime, one needs also to recognize that for many or most people it is possible to move from one stage to the next. Thus while the necessity for growth continues throughout a lifetime, the necessity to stay in a particular stage does not.

Dependence on teachers, programs, or movements may come from a diversity of conditions caused by an arrest in development or a situation resulting from underdeveloped or disabling circumstances. Dependence on teachers or groups or movements may also be the result of a cultural phenomena. Historically, cultures have spawned dependency through such institutions as monarchies, caste systems, arranged marriages, economic privileges, and state religions. On the other hand, many newer cultures, particularly societies based upon modern democracies, have spawned independence with elected leaders, equal opportunity, "free market" economies, marriages of choice, and open relationships.

Complete adulthood is the bridge within everyone that enables a person to cross over into the expanded awareness of a new way of living. Many in the past have crossed this bridge and have looked back compassionately at those still struggling. They want to help bridge the gap between child-adolescent dependency and adult independence in order to go on to expanded awareness. Inspired, they have established programs or movements and taught techniques designed to help others achieve the kind of realizations that allowed them to experience life in a newly expanded way.

Some personalities need more support than others, especially on the ego/emotional level. Some people are unwilling or unable to let go of defenses they have cultivated over many years. Expending so much of their energy defending themselves, they wind up in all sorts of difficult situations and problems. They need help. Their need is for guidance. Because of their need, teachers, programs, and movements, some rigidly organized and highly structured, prescribe specific actions for their followers.

Highly structured guidance can support people who are not yet independent enough to function and trust themselves regarding appropriate behavior and beliefs. They can be compared to physically arrested, underdeveloped, or disabled people, whose condition might necessitate nutritional counseling, an exercise group, or mechanical support devices such as crutches. There is no doubt of the actual need.

Someone who is intellectually arrested, underdeveloped, or disabled might need a reading specialist, a cognitive rehabilitation program, a tutor, or a course in critical thinking. The socially dependent might need structured recreation, a course in manners or interpersonal skills, a communal living support group. Those who are still dependent on the vocational/ financial level might need job training and placement, a course in money management, or even temporary welfare checks and food stamps. The need is obvious.

If someone is arrested, underdeveloped, or disabled morally or ethically, he or she might benefit from legal or social counseling, policing, and perhaps even rehabilitative imprisonment. Likewise, those who are ego/emotionally dependent and disturbed could benefit from individual or group therapy, a co-dependency support group, medication, or in-patient care. Again, there is no doubt of the necessity.

We are not saying that everyone who belongs to a support group or a movement or who follows a teacher is not an adult. There are many who come together with others to share, learn and grow in the most adult-like fashion. May they continue. We do, however, want to raise some questions that we think need to be asked and examined—disturbing as they might be. Not asking the questions could mean not knowing.

Are we dependent on a support group, movement, or teacher to such an extent that we can only "react" rather than "act?" If so, is our inner or outer life dry, dead, and without growth? Are we independent and adult enough not to impose our way on others as the best and only way? Is trust and confidence in ourselves and trust and confidence in the higher power (however we define it) growing together in our lives? Are we willing to face our fears, let go, and make the leap into the beyond on our own? These can be disturbing questions but questions whose answers can lead to growth. Here, too, each of us must make our own decision.

There are many people who would find the prospects of being on their own unappealing, perhaps because they are not ready to know or accept themselves as they are and go beyond. Not everyone is ready to handle responsibility for their own lives. Many still need the support and guidance of a variety of organized, structured approaches to life. To deny or dissuade them from reliance on systems is unwise.

At the same time, we need to recognize that increasingly more people are establishing themselves in adult independence, and that they are experiencing expanded awareness on their own. It is possible for them, like Thomas whom we described earlier, to proceed without unnecessary dependence on teachers, programs, and movements. Can not these same people trust their own intuition and the teacher within to guide them? We think so. They can still temporarily turn to others for help when it is needed and then once again continue on their own. Perhaps the time has come to go beyond accumulated knowledge, teachings, techniques, and authority in order to let the ego go completely and become established in awareness itself. Each person must decide for himself when he is ready to be on his own.

Does this mean that in the process of letting the ego go and becoming independent one has to live alone? Certainly not. It is perfectly reasonable to envision communities of like-minded, functioning adults who are together because they decide to share their talents and lives. Being an adult does not mean isolation, but rather sharing that is based not upon necessity, but rather upon desire, need, responsibility, and growth. Those who enjoy the company of others and those who are most creative and productive when working with others will naturally gravitate towards people who share that desire. Being "on your own" does not imply having to do everything in life alone nor does it necessitate giving up the company of those whose lives complement ours. Many of these people could be special teachers who appear at the time they are needed—a spouse, a friend, a child.

Far from advocating aloneness and the absence of loving relationships, we see all love as beginning with self-love. Being "on your own" implies a healthy self-concept or ego, self-confidence, self-esteem, and the absence of defenses that keep people separate from each other. Being firmly established in self-love puts one firmly in the position to be a "giver and sharer" in relationships rather than a "taker." Being on one's own often leads to a more compassionate outlook that moti-vates actions that benefit others.

We are convinced that no matter what a person's indi-vidual history may be, as everyone enters the next millennium more and more people will become independent adults and share the common experience of expanded awareness. This awareness is the result not of denying or destroying individu-ality, but rather of strengthening it to such a degree that it is possible to go beyond it and see clearly the oneness we all share.

Appendix
Quick Starts to
Independence

We have summarized the six major areas of growth and followed each summary with some specific suggestions for personal development in each of the major areas.

We recognize that these recommendations are geared primarily toward Americans and other western cultures with a heritage for independence, democratic political structures, and economies sufficiently prosperous that they can encourage opportunities for economic and personal freedom.

This qualification does not always apply for those who live under political, social, and economic oppression, nor for those who are physically or mentally disabled. Their difficulties are addressed in other forums and by other means. The recommendations can contribute to the development of adult independence.

The two most important principles that apply throughout **On Your Own** are:

1. Don't expect or allow others to do for you what you can do for yourself.

2. Accept the consequences of your own behavior without expecting or asking another to bail you out.

PHYSICAL INDEPENDENCE

On the most fundamental level, this means the ability to satisfy basic physical needs such as food, clothing, and shelter. On an advanced level, it is marked by responsibility for physical needs and behaviors as well as ability to maintain health, well-being, and physical development. Dependence on abusive substances, such as drugs or alcohol, or engaging in unsafe sexual practices, is definitely not the mark of a physically responsible adult.

Physically mature people can accept their bodies as they are, and they acknowledge their own strengths, limitations, or peculiar features. Whether they can or whether they even want to make an effort to change physically is not the issue. The issue is whether they accept themselves and the responsibility for themselves physically.

• Establish your own daily, healthy routine of rising, retiring, eating, relaxing, and exercising and stay with it without varying. Once it is established, you can be more flexible when necessary.

• Take it upon yourself to refrain from any abuse of drugs, alcohol, overeating, or irresponsible, unsafe sex. Seek help for yourself through therapy or such rehabilitation programs for any difficulties you can not manage yourself.

• Care for your own personal needs such as cleaning and organizing your living space.

• Don't live with your parents or invite your parents to live with you if other arrangements can be made.

• Question and refute any irrational "shoulds" you have in regard to living arrangements for yourself, your children, or elderly parents in light of today's availability of jobs, money, retirement benefits, and alternative housing.

INTELLECTUAL INDEPENDENCE

To different degrees, adults have the ability to use logic and to reason abstractly. They can deduce what will or will not happen if they take, or do not take, certain actions. They can also draw personal, but reasonable, conclusions about systems of belief. An adult intellect does not readily relinquish its independence and discrimination to become an uncritical tool to be used and exploited by a group or another individual. An adult intellect can appreciate the perspective of others with a degree of detachment, regardless of whether it accepts or rejects another's point of view.

• Sharpen and strengthen your powers of logic and critical thinking through reading, stimulating games, computer skills, continuing education.
• Apply the power of reason to all major decisions and conclusions you reach "intuitively."
• Engage yourself in stimulating discussions regarding such issues as politics, religion, and the environment, and put your opinions to the test of critical discussion.

SOCIAL INDEPENDENCE

Developed adults are generally able to meet and get along with other people while still retaining their own individuality. They do not use membership in a group to compensate for their own inability to interact socially. Rather they are contributing members of any group they belong to, while still retaining their own individuality and their ability to interact with the community and society in general.

When people in groups adopt a strict "we versus them" attitude, they can no longer perceive clearly or appreciate another's perspective. Their identity is completely absorbed in the identity of the group. They are not socially independent.

• Take the initiative in making your own friends or in belonging to groups of your own choosing.

• Face your social fears by participating in social events such as parties, dates, and community affairs. These fears aside, then opt to be alone when you decide.

• Allow yourself to experience what it is like to be alone by staying home by yourself more often. Try sleeping in an empty house or apartment.

• Be as honest with others as you can without being a "true confessor" or secret revealer.

• Rather than always doing what others are doing, do what you want to do and persuade them to come along.

MORAL DEVELOPMENT

Moral adults are characterized by an inner-directed, value-based sensitivity to other people and to the environment around them. Their values may be learned from parents, society, religion, or teachers, but those values have come to be their own. Individual conscience and responsibility underlie morality and action. But the values are personal and deeply felt, not superficial and blind, acting out of someone else's dictates.

Nothing sends the signal of moral immaturity more quickly than the self-righteous ravings of people telling others how to live their lives. The "black and white," "right and wrong" attitude of the morally immature indicates fixed, rigid, rebellious, fanatical, and adolescent-like moral dependence.

• Examine your own behavior to see that it is life-supporting and in accordance with such values as the Golden Rule: "Do unto others as you would have them do unto you."

• Don't engage in non-life supporting behavior and unfair practices just because they are "legal."

• Have the courage to drop or ease unreasonable moral sanctions or rules when you can see no harm done to all parties.

• Be willing to trust your own intuition or inner guide and accept the consequences with regard to your decisions.

• Seek out guidance from others whom you respect when you are in doubt whether an action is moral and responsible, rather than act impulsively or ignorantly.

VOCATIONAL/FINANCIAL RESPONSIBILITY

When people are vocationally independent, they have chosen a means of employment that they like and enjoy. They either have the skills to perform their chosen activity or they can learn the required skills. Also their vocational choice is practical in terms of money, demand, and geographical location. When someone does something he doesn't like or something which isn't economically in demand, or which he isn't qualified to do, he is vocationally dependent.

Able and competent adults are not regularly dependent on others for their financial resources, although they can accept help that is freely offered and does not undermine their development and independence. They do not trade their independence or integrity for someone's promises to take care of them financially. Financial, vocational and educational "entitlements" can stand in the way of being on their own.

• Get a job, any job for a starter, rather than wait for the best or most suitable job. Leave that job if a better or more preferable one presents itself.

• Provide your own food, clothing, and shelter, or make sufficient payment in work or money to those who provide it for you.

• If you are college students living away or if you live at home, then pay for or at least contribute to your own room and board.

• Pay all your own bills and accept the consequences if you don't even if it means repossession, eviction, bankruptcy, or ruined credit ratings, all of which are temporary setbacks that can be overcome.

• Change jobs, move to another area or acquire additional skills if you are dissatisfied or continually out of work. Seek vocational guidance, if necessary.

• Do not apply for or accept welfare benefits, food stamps, housing allowances unless you are genuinely in need of temporary or emergency assistance or you are physically or mentally handicapped.

• If you receive social security benefits or other retirement benefits, learn to get by on what you are granted or if you are able, work to earn more, if necessary. Accept no "special" benefits unless you are truly entitled to them or you are physically or mentally handicapped.

• Get loans to tide you over rough spots, but only if you can repay them yourself.

• Avoid jobs offered by relatives or friends unless you are certain you will be treated as impartially as any other employee.

• Seize the opportunity to start your own business if you are so inclined, and you can obtain legitimate backing.

EGO/EMOTIONAL INDEPENDENCE

People who have individuated into independent adults genuinely understand, accept, trust, and feel good about themselves as they are. However, people with dependent emotionality and egos are vulnerable people. They need to constantly defend themselves just like a weakened or wounded soldier needs to be excessively on guard. Failure to individuate on the ego/emotional level results in defensive behaviors which are used unconsciously to defend weakened egos. These behaviors include blaming, excuse making, attacking, avoiding, and scapegoating, to name a few. These ego defensive behaviors are associated with fear, anger, guilt, and jealousy.

Separation-individuation is not complete in people who are fearful or unable to control, moderate, or even get through emotional dilemmas. Because their egos are so vulnerable, they get severely upset when things don't work out the way they want. They don't believe in their own ability to get through emotional difficulties. The ego is what they have been defending all the time—a collection of thoughts they have about themselves—that ironically, they can change. Successful separation-individuation on the ego/emotional level is characterized by people with a learned confidence in their own ability to face both challenge and denial.

We are often asked, "What can I do to become ego/emotionally independent?" Over the years the notion of doing something made less and less sense and the concrete or specific suggestions seemed more vacuous. Because becoming independent egoically and emotionally was more related to a process than a content, the question of doing something was more and more difficult to conceptualize. Certainly becoming independent in all the above areas does help, but what can we do directly on the ego/emotional level? Go back to Chapter Three to review and become comfortable using the eight-point guidelines for effective assertion, the six simple steps to help alleviate misunderstandings in irksome situations, and the effective ways of handling anger and frustration. Here are some other ways to process yourself:

•Communicate openly and honestly with yourself. Don't hide your underlying feelings and desires from yourself, no matter what they are. Ask yourself, "What do I really feel?" or "What do I really fear?" It may be painful, but it is worth the effort. A good friend, counselor, or therapist may provide the confrontation you need and facilitate the necessary catharsis.

• Understand not only your strengths, but also your weaknesses. Contrary to popular misconceptions, our personalities are not miraculously transformed into perfection as we grow to adulthood. We are merely better able to benefit from our strengths and less plagued by our weaknesses. Certain tendencies are and always will be part of our life-time traits. We can, however, try to figure out where our weaknesses have come from, how they are affecting us now, and what will happen if

we don't understand them sufficiently to overcome their negative influence in our lives. Read all you can about such matters
and objectively listen to what others are telling you.

• Accept yourself as you are right now. Accept your
strengths and your weaknesses. Remember that acceptance
does not mean that we agree or like our weaknesses. Learn to
be still with yourself through such techniques as meditation,
breathing exercises, biofeedback, or progressive relaxation.
After you have established some stillness, take a few moments
and silently repeat to yourself, "I am who I am and that's all
who I am right now, no matter what anybody says or thinks."
Dare to feel and believe it.   At first it doesn't seem to fit
because you have been telling yourself the opposite for so
long—"I'm not good enough," or "I should be better than I am"
or "I'm not OK because others think or say so." Just for a
moment believe it so for yourself. Only one touch with it will
go right through you. Allow yourself to think it for a moment
anytime it comes to you during the day. In this way, you begin
to reprogram your concept about yourself. After all a self-
concept is the thoughts you have about yourself.

• Take the gamble or risk to let go and be yourself with
yourself and with others. Perhaps this will mean for you that
you engage in more self-disclosure. Be yourself and recognize
the creative power of your own thoughts. Know that the ego
you have been defending is nothing more than the thoughts you
have about yourself and that the essential you goes beyond any
and all thoughts.

BIBLIOGRAPHY

Adelson, J. "The Mystique of Adolescence." *Psychiatry*, Summer, 1, (1964): 1-5.

Allport, G. *Pattern and Growth in Personality*. NY: Holt, Rinehart & Winston, 1961.

American Psychiatric Association: *Diagnostic and Statistical Manual of Mental Disorders* (3rd ed. rev.). Washington, DC: American Psychiatric Association, 1987.

Bocknek, Gene, *The Young Adult: Development After Adolescence*. CA: Brooks/Cole, 1980.

Boyer, E. L. *College: The Undergraduate Experience in America*. NY: Harper & Row, 1987.

Cardelle, Frank D. *Youth and Adult: The Shared Journey Toward Wholeness*. NY: Gardner, 1989.

Coleman, James S. *Youth: Transition to Adulthood* ("Report of the Panel on Youth of the President's Science Advisory Committee, 1972.") Chicago: University of Chicago, 1974.

Ellis, A. *Reason and Emotion in Psychotherapy*. NY: Lyle Stuart, 1962.

Erikson, E. *Childhood and Society*. NY: Norton, 1950.

Erikson, E. "Identity and the Life Cycle." *Psychological Issues*, 1, (1959): 1-171.

Erikson, E. "Reflections on the Dissent of Contemporary Youth." *Inter national Journal of Psychoanalysis*, 51, (1970): 11-22.

Fish, Betty, and Raymond Fish. *A Parent's Guide To Letting Go*. VA: Betterway Publication, 1988.

Fletcher, Joseph. *Moral Responsibility: Situation Ethics in Action*. Philadelphia: Westminster, 1967.

Fromm, E. *The Art of Loving*. NY: Harper, 1956.

Gallagher, B.J. "Ascribed and Self-Reported Attitude Differences Between Generations." *Pacific Sociological Review*. 19, (1976): 317-332.

Giddan, Norman, Sally Vallongo. *Parenting Through the College Years*. VT: Williamson, 1988.

Glenn, H. Stephen, and Jane Nelsen. *Raising Self Reliant Children in a Self-Indulgent World*. CA: Prima Publ. & Communications, 1988.

Gordon, Thomas. *P.E.T.—Parent Effectiveness Training*. NY: Wyden, 1970.

Gross, Jane. "More Young Single Men Hang Onto Apron Strings." *The New York Times*, 16 June 1991.

Havighurst, R. *Developmental Tasks and Education*. London: Longmans, Gree, 1952.

Hawley, Richard A. *The Big Issues in the Adolescent Journey*. NY, Walker, 1988.

Jung, C. [The Stages of Life.] In R. Hull (trans.), *The Structure and Dynamics of the Psyche (2nd ed.)*. Princeton, NJ: Princeton University Press, 1969.

Kernberg, O. "Early Ego Integration and Object Relations." *Annals of the New York Academy of Sciences*. 193, (1972): 233-247.

Kohlberg, Lawrence. *The Psychology of Moral Development.*
      San Francisco: Harper and Row, 1984.
Kutner, L. "Parent & Child," *The New York Times.* 23 May 1991.
Lancaster, J.B., J. Altmann, A.S. Rossi, and L.R. Sherrod (eds.) *Parenting
      Across the Life Span: Biosocial Dimensions.* NY: Gruyter,
      1987.
Levinson, D., C. Darrow, E. Klein, M. Levinson, and B. McKee. *The
      Seasons of a Man's Life.* NY: Knopf, 1978.
Lerner, R.M., and J.R. Knapp. "Actual and Perceived Intergenerational
      Attitudes of Late Adolescents and Their Parents." *Journal of
      Youth and Adolescents.* 4,(1975): 17-36.
Loevinger, J. *Ego Development.* San Francisco: Jossey-Bass, 1976.
Marcia, J. "Ego-Identity Status: Relationship to Change in Self-Esteem,
      'General Malajustment,' and Authoritarianism." *Journal of
      Personality,* 35, (1967): 118-133.
Maslow, A. *Motivation and Personality.* NY: Harper, 1954.
Maslow, A. *Toward a Psychology of Being.* Princeton, NJ: Van Nostrand,
      1962.
Masterson, James F. *The Narcissistic and Borderline Disorders.* NY:
      Brunner/Mazel, 1981.
Piaget, J. "Piaget's Theory." In P.H. Mussen, (Ed.), *Carmichael's Manual
      of Child Psychology* (3rd. ed.). NY: Wiley, 1, (1970): 703-732.
Peck, R. "Psychological Developments in the Second Half of Life." In W.
      Sze (Ed.), *Human Life Cycle.* NY: Jason Aronson, 1975.
Rappaport, L. *Personality Development.* Glenview, IL: Scott, Foresman,
      1972.
Shedler, Jonathan, and Jack Block. "Adolescent Drug Use and
      Psychological Health: A Longitudinal Inquiry." *American
      Psychologist.* 45, 5, (1990): 612-630.
Stallone, James, and Sy Migdal. *Growing Sane.* PA: Upshur Press, 1991.
Symonds, P. *From Adolescent to Adult.* NY: Columbia University Press,
      1961.
White, R. *Lives in Progress* (3rd ed.). NY: Holt, Rinehart & Winston,
      1975. (1st ed. 1952.)
Wittenberg, R. *Postadolescence.* NY: Gune & Stratton, 1968.
York, Phyllis and David, and Ted Wachte. *Toughlove.* NY: Bantam
      Books, 1982.

Index

A

Abortion, 131-134
Acceptance, 66-70, 132-140
Alcohol Abuse, 148-153
Anger, 69-70, 81-84, 92, 110,
 129-131, 172
Arrested Growth, 4-6, 8-9
Assertion, 67-71, 129-131,
Awareness, 173-181
 disturbances accompanying,
 177-180

C

Co-dependency, 22-23
Coping, 67-68, 82-84, 135-140,
 160-163, 165-168, 172, 176
Criminal Behavior, 146-148
Crisis at Retirement 168-170

D

Depression, 57, 92, 155-159,
 164-168
Disabling Physical Illness,164-168
Dropping Out, 145-146
Drug Abuse, 148-153

E

Ego, 40, 172, 178-9, 186
Emotions, 40, 172
Entitlement, 10-12, 14-18, 36-39,
 88-92, 106-107

F

Fear of Abandonment, 65-67, 89,
 108, 116-119, 140-145, 179
 of Failure, 116-119, 152, 172
Forgiveness, 144-145
Foreclosure, 90-91
Four "A's" (assault, addiction,
 adultery, abandonment), 77-78,
 127, 141, 148-153, 163

G

Guilt, 55-56, 65-67, 74-75, 79,
 110, 140-145, 152, 160-163,
 172, 174

H

Homosexuality, 134-140

I

Identity,46-50, 69, 89-91, 100
Independence:
 physical, 27-30,
 intellectual, 30-31
 social, 31-33,
 moral/ethical, 33-36,
 vocational/financial, 36-39,
 75-76, 88-99, 106-114,
 119-122
 ego/emotional, 40-41, 88-91, 174
 quick steps, Appendix

L

Living Will, 79-80, 112

M

Mental Health Problems, 153-164
 psychosis, 154-155
 depression, 155-157, 159
 suicide, 157-164

P

Personality Disorders 52-58
 borderline, 52
 dependent, 53
 passive/aggressive, 53-54
 narcissist, 55-57
Pregnancy 127-134
Protracted Adolescence, 5-6,
 10-12, 13-14, 22-23, 26-27,
 44-46, 61, 100-106, 119-122,
 161-162

R

Regressed Behavior, 4-6, 9-10,
 166-168
Rebellion, 12-13, 30-31, 34,
 44-46, 59, 64, 123-124, 142,
 146-147
Relationship difficulties, 122-127,

S

"Sacred Cows", 19-21
Sandwich Generation, 80-82,
Separation-individuation 26-27,
 40-46, 50-61, 90-91, 102,
 126-127, 173, 180-186,

Index of Illustrative Cases

Chapter/Page		Identification	Illustrative Case
1	3	Hugo	Ego/emotional Dependency
1	8	Marcia	Arrested Growth
1	9	Mildred	Regressed Behavior
1	13	Ruth	Protracted Parenting
2	29	Widow/son	Physical Dependency
2	32	Cynthia	Social Dependency
2	35	Paul	Moral Dependency
2	38	College Couple	Vocational/Financial
2	43	same	Ego/Emotional Dependency
			Personality Disorders
2	52	General	Borderline
2	53	General	Dependent
2	53	General	Passive-Agressive
2	56	Sara	Narcissist
2	58	Mother/daughter	Guilt; Financial Dependency
3	64	David & Martha	Coping: Children at Home
3	74	College Dropout	Guilt and Fear
3	79	Disabled Mother	Parenting Parents
3	80	Genevieve & Sam	Sandwich Generation/ Double Dependency
3	83	Father-in-law	Coping with Anger
4	98	College Senior	Avoidance of Separation
4	99	Joe	Guilt; Vocational Independence
4	105	Daughter at home	Uncontrolled Spending

4	108	Grace & Peter	Ego/Emotional & FinancialDependency
4	112	Ann	Depression/Fear/ Financial Insecurity
5	116	Mother/daughter	Fear of Abandonment
5	123	Father/daughter	Fear of Failure/ Dependency
5	126	Married son/parents	Ego/Emotional; Vocational Social Dependency
5	129	Karen & Trudy	Unplanned Pregnancy
5	133	Barbara	Abortion; Individuation
5	138	Allen	Homosexuality; Acceptance
5	141	General	Running Away
5	146	General	Dropping out
5	147	Gene	Criminal Behavior; Ego/ Emotional Dependency
5	151	Denise & Jan	Protracted Parenting; Substance Abuse
5	158	Tim & Sara	Suicide; Ego/Emotional Dependency
5	161	Debra & Grant	Protracted Adolescence; Suicide Threats
5	164	Veronica	Disabling Physical
5	165	John	Illness & Depression
6	174	Angelica	Expansion of Awareness; Ego/ Emotional Dependency
6	181	Thomas	Expansion of Awareness; Teacher/ Movement Dependency